I HATE

YOUR FACE

**(And Other Things I Wish I Could
Tell My Coworkers)**

Connie O'Reyes

www.connieoreyes.com

Cover design by Erin Neises

Copyright 2018 by C. Castellucci

Published 2018, Chicago, IL

ISBN- 978-1-7323703-1-9 (Paperback)

ISBN- 978-1-7323703-0-2 (Ebook)

AUTHOR'S NOTE

Hi! Thank you for reading this book. I put a lot of work into it and hope you love it as much as I love you for reading it. Please note, self-publishing is super hard, so if you find any grammar errors, please pretend they don't exist. Also, people in this book are real. Some have their names their mama's gave them, some do not. I use a lot of hyperbole, but know that the stories, while true, are my personal opinion. (I had to put that in here so no one sues or fires me. You'll soon see why.)

DEDICATION

To: Mom & Papa

From: C.O.R. I

Sorry for all the bad words.

CONTENTS

1. Power Suits and Prostitutes 1

2. The Flying O'Reyes Sisters 16

3. The Story of Box Mountain and Best Friends 29

4. The Ecosystem of a Family Friendly Restaurant ...42

5. Discounted Pajama Pants 56

6. File Bicycle Shorts Under 'S' for 'Smelly 68

7. Office Translator 81

8. Stale Doughnuts and Career Paths 86

9. Market Research and Evil Villains 99

10. Bathroom Break 117

11. Watch Out for the Antelopes 122

12. Why the State of Illinois is Going Bankrupt 137

13. 12a Floors of Anxiety, A Play 152

14. Will Run for Blog 157

15. Six Month Review 173

16. Poop Stories of Love 175

17. Death and the CTA 188

18. A Field Trip to Bourbon Street 201

19. Beware the Leather Jacket 220

20. Carrie Bradshaw is a Liar 226

21. The Ann Taylor Loft Suit Strikes Again 240

22. When I Grow Up 247

23. Random Words of Wisdom I Wanted to Leave You
    With Before I Leave This Meeting 260

24. Exit Interview 263

Acknowledgments 267

Power Suits and Prostitutes

JOB INTERVIEWS ARE the WORST.

The only difference between an interview and prostitution is that one of them ends in guaranteed payment (provided of course that your pimp is a real go-getter). I hate job interviews because in the short allotted time, you are supposed to wow, capture, and hook an interviewer right off the bat. You are solely responsible for selling yourself as a confident, problem-solving, gold star candidate that is well qualified to meet your potential boss's wildest fantasies. The same goes with prostitution- but at least in that field, you don't have to spend the entire time in uncomfortable hosiery. And you definitely don't have to wear power suits.

The same can almost be said for the opening chapter in one's first book. Sure, you feel confident that you can eventually get your audience to fall in love with your unique sense of wit- but how can you pull it off in the first scene, when they can't even see the brand new, discounted Ann Taylor Loft suit you have on? Luckily, I've kept the tags on and tucked them into my shirt collar so that I can easily return it in case this first chapter falls to shit. Since I've never done this before, I guess I'll have to rely on the job interview format and pull from some standard interviewing questions to make this easier on both of us.

Tell me a little bit about yourself.

Oh this is a good question. But where should I begin? Perhaps by starting off with something like, "I have documented evidence via a VHS home movie that proves I was a child genius because I could recite ALL the lyrics to Jingle Bells at the age of 3. That's right, bells on bobtail ring!" Or should I jump ahead a little bit to current events, trying to think of a creative way to say that since entering the workforce, I've been using all my sick days to sit at home and watch *Gilmore Girls* reruns while eating dinosaur shaped chicken nuggets with my dog Chompers?

I guess it'd be best to give you a background story. Since you already called me in for this interview, it must mean you have some interest in my life (or that you have already read all the celebrity memoirs covering up this book on the store shelf, in which case; hello!)

I was born on the awesome streets of Chicago. My parents grew up around Wrigley Field, where the Northside baseball team the Chicago Cubs play, and where twenty-year-olds now go to get wasted. My grandparents were Irish (my mom) and Mexican (my dad), making my younger sister and me the whitest Latinas you will ever see. Because I was second generation Irish, it was seventeen years before my high school friend Kathleen (The last of thirteen kids in her family- I spent most of Spanish class asking her details about the bathroom situation in her house and if she could even name all her siblings. She could!) kindly explained to me that the reason my head was so big was because it was "an Irish thing." She failed to mention that along with giant heads comes great stubbornness and a tendency to burn in the sun faster than a vampire, but I figured these things out on my own eventually.

On the other side of things, I have a distant, yet loyal connection to my Mexican side. One time though, at a family party filled with mariachi bands and tamales, my ethnicity was tested- and I failed. Miserably. At this particular fiesta, my great uncle shouted over to me "Mija! Come say hello to your uncle!" Mija of course, being the endearing term for a young girl, short for 'mi hija' or 'my daughter' in Spanish (and now you know as much Spanish as I do).

I however had no clue what this man was saying to me since my father only tried to teach me Spanish once in a twisted childhood game. While stopped at a red light, he would close his eyes in the left turn lane, and only open them to move the car if I correctly said 'verde,' which is green in Spanish (as you may know if you ever ordered salsa from Chipotle which did not exist when I was a kid). Frightened that we would get rear-ended, I would start to scream 'GO!,' thinking cars would crash into us, not knowing the rules of the road or that he wasn't closing his eyes all the way.

You could see now the reason for my confusion when my great uncle started throwing out Spanish words in his attempt to call me over. After the third try, I looked around worried thinking, I don't know who this Mija girl is, but she better come over because he is getting really pissed. Luckily, my dad caught sight of this and brought me over to sub in for 'Mija' and appease my uncle, who had moved on to more important things like cutting up his own hot peppers he brought to the party in his sport coat. Being a shy child, these parties would often terrify me as there were tons of people, yet there was always someone's birthday to celebrate, hence a giant birthday cake, so I prevailed. Viva la cake!

To put a name on the greatest combination of ethnicities to date, when I was born my parents (or as I imagine: my dad having one too many celebratory PBRs and my mom loopy with post-birthing exhaustion) gave me a middle name starting with an O that could be used in combination with our last name resulting in the greatness that is "O'Reyes." My sister has the same deal, so if you ever see an O'Reyes in the news for kicking over a liquor store, chances are it was her! She's the bad one! (Sidenote: Mom, one time Caitlyn had a party at our house and her friend puked in the sink. I have no idea who provided her the alcohol.) (Double sidenote: Haha Caitlyn! Mom and Papa now love me more!)

Work experiences were always visible in my family. My dad continued his dad's law firm, and I have lots of fond memories of going to work with him. Law is one of the older professions that require things like file cabinets with legal briefs and secretaries who file them away. I mainly remember that we got to color with highlighters and make Xerox copies of our hands, which is exactly what I do now in my office, except now I also take breaks to go shopping on Amazon.

My mom, on the other hand, had several various jobs, with the common theme of helping people, accompanied by many, many years in school. Both of these things could be contributing factors to why my sister and I sometimes refer to her affectionately as 'crazy,' and why when it was time for me to search for a profession, I chose a job that would lead to free highlighters and file cabinets. But both of my parents' seamless work ethic is also why at 16, I promptly walked over to the nearest Walgreens and asked for a job application. *Because that's what O'Reyes' do- they work!* (Sidenote: How are you pronouncing that in your head right now? Try, 'oh-ray-S-ez'. It's difficult with the s' at the end; luckily I am here to help you out.)

Another thing O'Reyes' do is shovel snow. With two girls and no brothers, there was no opportunity for sexism. At our house, the snow certainly wasn't going to shovel itself, so us girls were assigned the task. Not having boys around was cool in that it allowed me to work for my damn self, and made me realize I needed no man to pay my bills! (Flips hair fiercely like Beyoncé.) But seriously, parents, you want to know how to keep your daughter (or son for that matter) off the pole? Make them shovel snow and take out the trash. Those are two viable professions right there.

Moving on with this Dickensian rant, I spent the first 12 years of my life in a Catholic school uniform, which is my argument as to why I still can't properly accessorize. (Rosaries are a prayer tool, not a necklace!) I have a best friend (and two others who are going to be pissed they didn't get a full chapter about them in here. Sorry Cara and Emily! Love you!) who I have known since kindergarten, which you will read more about later. She helped me meet this one guy who took me to a homecoming dance in high school, and I clenched my nails into him good, and got him to marry me. He often says the craziest things. Examples: "No we cannot watch Twilight for the hundredth time, *stop watching that movie, you are not eleven!*" "Why does the dog have a hoodie on? Take it off. *Because he's a dog!*" "No, you cannot watch football with me. Why? *Because you keep saying that the quarterback looks constipated and probably needs to go to the bathroom!*" He's weird. But one time he had to pull out a deceased rabbit that had crawled into our dryer vent, so I enjoy keeping him around for his magic tricks.

Some other notable things about my past are as follows:

- When I was four, my Auntie Di locked herself out while babysitting me and I unlocked the door and let her back inside. I don't recall this but it is told every Thanksgiving and you would have thought I cured leprosy the way my family retells this tale.

- I won a poetry contest in third grade and won a dozen bagels. My mom was THRILLED. Her excitement for free bagels may very well be what motivated me to become a writer.

- In sixth grade, I was moved up to first chair in the school band because I had mad clarinet skills. I have done nothing with this skill since.

- I made zero friends at college, but I commuted, and it's hard making friends with crazy people on a public train.

- I successfully ran the 2010 Chicago marathon without pooping my pants (which is a thing that can happen when you run 26.2 miles) and I have been carb-loading for the next race ever since.

- I constantly think in numbers, like how if I finish this chapter I will be 4.3% finished writing this book. (I'm not Rain Man though; I had to use a calculator.)

Describe your previous work experience.

Well that's exactly what this book is all about! Please, read on!

However, if you're looking for some self-help book on how to be a successful business person, making the 30 under 30 Forbes list, you're SOL. But don't stop reading! I'm not a total lost cause either. I went to a large private Midwestern college, graduated in Marketing, and even got a minor in Sales Leadership. (But in full disclosure, that was to get the $500 stipend that didn't have to go towards tuition and went straight into the late night Wendy's post-drinking fund.) From there, I worked at four significant marketing jobs, all of which you will hear about later, but what you need to know now is that it wasn't spent in a soul-searching, 'Eat, Pray, Love' inner quest for fulfillment. My mottos for work thus far in life have been, "F- bitches, make money." from the famous rapper the Notorious B.I.G. and "It's a PowerPoint, not freaking heart surgery." from a brilliant former coworker, respectively.

And for you non-businessy types, (who probably know enough about business not to use the word businessy) don't worry about not being able to relate to these stories. This isn't about nonsense business jargon that no one understands like 'streamlined processes' or 'work ethic.' Rather, it's about the encounters with strange coworkers, awkward situations that come with learning a new job, and scary career decisions one is forced to make way too early on in life that can well impact their future. You know, the type of shit that makes everyone in any profession drink the alcohol.

Do you have any personal hobbies?

Yes! You are holding it. I like writing.

Somewhere during my second job post-college, I got incredibly bored and started a blog. Then later I started another blog where I documented my misfit adventures in learning to run, ending in a marathon. It was then that I realized a few things: 1. I really liked to write. 2. I really, really liked people telling me they liked my writing. And 3. You can find the time to create and write a blog if you have the determination to ignore your work to-do list.

Also? I have a passion for being lazy. I would say it goes beyond a hobby into a true, well-trained skill that took years to develop. I often sit at work wondering how I could get a medical job where they would put me in a coma forty hours a week to study brain patterns. That would be heaven. Sleep all day, go home, and watch TV? Sign me up! My mom used to think I had anemia and would make me take Flintstone vitamins until she realized no, this one is just gifted. I could probably have written this book a lot sooner if it hadn't been for all the awesome re-runs that are on during the day. On any given sick day, I can be entertained from 10 AM to 5 PM with a nice medley of *Gilmore Girls*, *Roseanne*, *Will & Grace*, *The Big Bang Theory*, *and Frasier* (to educate myself). If I'm not too tired, I can even stay awake for a late-night *Friends* marathon too. Man, I love TV.

Tell me a little about your work ethic.

I was eight the first time I was caught slacking off on the job by my boss. It was in front of my house, where my neighbors and I had our shop set up- warm lemonade for the low, low price of fifty cents. We had priced it just right so that unsuspecting suckers would feel compelled to leave the dollar for the four sweet girls growing a business. Apple could have learned a thing or two from us.

I was at the counter waiting for any potential customers to walk down Francisco Street, which was unlikely since our neighbor Mrs. Jennings had already gone out for her afternoon errands and Mr. Beaudion had already stopped by earlier. Other than those two neighbors, hardly anyone came down our tree-lined street in the Irving Park neighborhood of the city.

I was growing restless, hot from the humidity that summer which had me sporting my lime green culottes and a t-shirt with a screen print of neon paint splatters. Thirsty, I debated whether it was worth the risk of going inside and getting roped into cleaning- a vicious threat from my mom whenever we wandered inside. Looking back, she was a genius. Although we didn't have the tidiest house on the block, (holiday preparation always included taking shifts from our screaming mother who needed all the laundry baskets to be *put away right now or else she's throwing out all the Christmas presents!*) using a messy house as a constant threat to be used at her disposal was probably the only way my mother ever got any peace and quiet. Now I'm wondering if she's really crazy, or just brilliant.

My coworkers at the stand consisted of my sister Caitlyn, who was four at the time, and essentially useless other than using her cuteness to draw in some customers. Nicole was the younger of the two Kessler sisters, our across-the-street neighbors. She was also useless yet adorable. And then there was Ann. Ann was the Kessler version of me- the oldest of two girls, smart, creative, and also a fabulous dresser, often sporting culottes herself. We had just finished our morning business meeting outlining specific rules on work schedules and product scarcity (my mom only had half a container left of Country Time lemonade powder for us to use.) Not too long after though, I started drinking a cup of the merchandise. Even though the sun melted our ice supply away, it was a nice change from hose water. Hours (or perhaps minutes) passed when I went for another. It was on the third cup that Ann started to notice.

"Haven't you had a cup already?" She said sternly. Being the eldest out of all of us, I usually followed Ann's instructions out of respect for the first-born rank. But as the temperature grew, my respect for authority faded. The heat was morphing my opinion of Ann from summertime best friend to a ruthless sales manager, keeping us in the hot sun to shill out her crappy product. "We aren't going to make any money if you drink all the lemonade!"

Really? Even though she had two years of math classes on me, I could still do a quick scan of our financial status. Our supplies were given to us by our parents- old Solo cups from a previous BBQ and one scoop of Country Time powder. Added together, adjusting for inflation, our overhead costs equated to the tip Mrs. Jennings left, minus the hugs.

"I'll just have my mom make another batch." I replied, un-phased by Ann's growing concern. Our support staff had already quit, giving up hope on making the Crain's Best Small Business list and instead focused their time on the coveted pink Skip-It. I knew though that if a big rush order came in, we could send one of them into the house for a quick refill.

Angered, I could see Ann's patience with me was fading. It was the face I would see many other times again at my first job after college, but I didn't care. I knew nothing great would come from peddling warm crappy lemonade to a handful of neighbors, and I knew it didn't matter how much leftover we had, we weren't going to strike rich or be famous from a lame lemonade stand, so I gave up. A trend I'd see many times over when faced with a shitty job that was leading nowhere.

Worried about maintaining our friendship, and not wanting to lose out on the opportunity to try out her brand new moon shoes later, I avoided confrontation. "I have to go to the bathroom!" I shouted, grabbed Caitlyn, and headed inside to hide upstairs in our parents' room and watch TV but not before finishing my cup and tossing it aside on the grass.

Last I heard, Ann went on to become a Senior Associate Director for an Entrepreneurship Center at a large top rated Institution. I went on to find that cold beer tastes one million times better in red Solo cups than warm lemonade.

What are your goals?

I have two.

1. Work goal:

I want to become a manager someday in marketing research, so I can mentor young up-and-comers like me someday. I would make them sit in my office as I sit behind my large cherry wood desk, like the kind you see in Presidents' old houses. Inhaling coffee vapor fumes from my futuristic coffee machine (because it's in the future you know) I'd give sage advice, or perhaps read cautionary tales of things to avoid in the workplace from this very book.

Also, I'd like to have a position someday that pays me enough money for me to comfortably afford monthly parking in downtown Chicago, thus avoiding the pee-scented cesspool that is the CTA (Chicago Transit Authority). Not having to sit next to someone in a crowded train car while they clip their toenails? *That's* how I'll know I've made it.

2. Writing goal:

I have this goal all carefully planned out since I often fantasize about it on my train commute.

First, I will write this book. If you are reading it now, it's a good sign that I've done it. Next, I get it published online because that is the way this industry is going and Amazon is making it super easy for me to become the next J.K. Rowling (Accio-bestseller list!).

Then, I will throw the greatest, most epic, fantastically awesome book launch party of the century. Magically, as soon as the book is printed I will drop down to my goal weight, fitting into a black lace, long-sleeved, backless, mid-thigh length dress that I bought for $16.00 at Marshalls. It will be such a special night that I'll even wash *and* dry my hair. Maybe even curl it, *who knows*, it might be that insane. The book launch party will be at a huge fancy bar downtown with a split staircase in the center, which I will successfully walk down in heels, even though when I currently walk in any sort of heel over 2 inches, I look like a man trying on his girlfriend's shoes drunk, walking down a cobblestone street. Everyone I ever meet will be there, cheering me on as the DJ announces my debut on the New York Times Best Seller list, knocking out whatever dumbass celebrity memoir is currently out. From there, we would all break out into a dance party with all the best 90s songs. I would be dancing like a Fly Girl just like the dancers from In Living Color. Then, my favorite author of all time, Jen Lancaster, humor memoir goddess herself, would break out into a dance battle with me, where we would all finish by cheers-ing our fancy drinks in midair.

(Freeze frame, 80s movie style).

Is that not the best goal you have ever heard? I hope it is enough to get you to keep reading, if not for your personal interest in these stories, but for the chance of making a young woman's dream of shaking her ass like a Fly Girl at her very own book launch party come true.

Why should we hire you? (Alternatively, why should we read your book?)

Because I would like to buy ice cream. And a new hoodie for my dog!

To wrap this up and give you the final push of why you should hire me as your entertainer for the next twenty-four chapters, I'll leave you with my elevator pitch. In job hunting, you are supposed to have a five-second statement that can easily illustrate everything you want to convey to a prospective employer, apparently in the rare chance you are on an elevator together. Here is an example:

Hey Mr. Walters- my name is Jimmy Bob, and I am a Regional VP at Jimmy Bob's Hot Dogs! We sell top-rated hot dog and hot dog products and I would like to show your company the Jimmy Bob way through hard work and by earning your trust. Would you like to buy some hot dogs today?

I would bet my 2005 Toyota Rav4 that no one has ever used an elevator pitch in an elevator. It is way too small of a space to speak to someone let alone sell yourself. That would be like ending a first date with a closing line like, "I think my soulmate is sitting in this car." Who does that? Fortunately, I cannot see your reaction, unless you are reading this book on a train in Chicago, in which case there is a good chance I am awkwardly standing next to you waiting for an opportunity to ask "ISN'T IT GREAT??!!" But if you aren't, pretend you are standing in an elevator with me. Here is my pitch:

Hi there! My name is Connie O'Reyes and I've been mentally punching coworkers in the throat since I was old enough to work. I'd like to tell you lots of funny stories about annoying coworkers, embarrassing mishaps in the workplace, and my overall journey from being a marketing student to having my very own office where I can close the door and watch YouTube videos during my lunch break. Would you please read the rest of this book?

Are you awkwardly staring straight at the elevator buttons, wishing the doors would open so you can leap out? No? Excellent! That's good to hear.

And with that, it seems as if I have successfully made it to the end of the interview without you noticing my sweat stains or letting out a nervous fart. In real job interviews, it can often be the only make or break opportunity to sell yourself to a boss and land that dream job. Luckily, when you write a book, you can add as many chapters as you want for the long sell, or as prostitutes call it, swooning the Jon. So with that, here are the most horrific, awkward, comically, self-deprecating stories about my journey of becoming an average, mildly successful businesswoman, or at least one that doesn't come to work hungover anymore. Enjoy!

(Stands up, shakes hand awkwardly, and then proceeds to wander around the office floor frantically looking for the exit so she can run to the nearest *McDonald's* restroom and vomit.)

The Flying O'Reyes Sisters

ONE OF THE MOST DIFFICULT management positions I've come across is being a big sister. And admittedly, one of the best employees to ever have is a little sister. What I'm trying to get at is, I'm an awesome big sister, and Caitlyn, my little sister, isn't so bad either.

I was born in the year 1985, when the Chicago Bears won the Super Bowl and, much like the Bears franchise, I have been touting it as the best year in history ever since. From what I can tell by pictures and retold family stories of my youth, I was a happy, albeit shy child. I liked to cling to my mother and made her carry me around in Wiggle Worms class during singing and dancing time even though all the other three-year-olds were on the ground socializing and networking. Still, life was good, and the golden pillow I sat atop every day was pretty cozy.

Then tragedy struck.

In 1989, Taylor Swift was born, and so was my sister. I know Taylor Swift was born that year because of her album. I know Caitlyn was born this year because that is the day my golden pillow was swiped out from under me. To give you a sense of my world BC (Before Caitlyn), there is a picture shoved in a family album somewhere of me as an ADORABLE four-year-old, grinning from ear to ear, sitting on my mom's lap the night before Caitlyn arrived. Caitlyn sensed that I was blissfully happy that night and decided to pop out two months early, crushing my comfortable life as the only person sitting on my mom's lap. After Caitlyn was born, my family never took a picture of me again.

That's not entirely true, but I think it established the dramatic effect of having a new sibling crash the party and disrupt your family circle.

Caitlyn was a preemie, which is hilarious for a few reasons. As an adult, she now stands as a ten-foot giant, and even though I am only five feet, six inches and a quarter, I still maintain that I am taller than her. A few months after she was born, my parents let me sit in on a family picture, and there is a Sears portrait somewhere of the four of us- my dad with his signature mustache, my mom with an 80's perm and some outfit that looked something like Victorian England meets working girl (love you mom), me, the bell of the ball, and Caitlyn no-neck- the fattest baby ever to roll the earth.

Whenever I need to laugh, I think of this picture. She has no visible sighting of any space between her third chin and her bulging belly, her eyes are popping out as if the photographer is holding up a bottle in the distance, and her hair is a matted mess. Next to her is me- a well-proportioned, perfectly groomed child with bangs that fall perfectly over my forehead and a smile that would make anyone want to have kids.

That description of baby ogre Caitlyn might sound cruel and heartless, but that's how we love each other. I make fun of her, and she, in turn, gets me back in some evil way, like becoming adorable.

Caitlyn was an evil genius early on, and at an early age would pull my hair so hard I remember the pain it would cause to this day. I would scream at her, but my mom would say pithy things like, "she's just a baby." She was no baby- she was an evil monster sent down to destroy my thick beautiful hair.

When she wasn't pulling out my tresses, Caitlyn took to calling me 'cocky' as her dumbed-down, baby variation of Connie. This was fine with me until my aging Irish Grandma, who had a hearing aid, caught on and thought she was calling me 'caca,' which means 'shit' in Spanish. (Sidenote: If you take the Spanish words in this chapter and combine it with our Spanish lesson from chapter one, you have *caca verde*, which means, green shit. You're welcome). So on a given visit to Grandma's, you'd have a baby calling me cocky and a Grandma calling me caca. Needless to say, my ego was severely bruised at a young age and has never quite recovered.

Despite the name calling and hair torture, from the point that Caitlyn was born, I no longer was the carefree child. I was a big sister, a responsibility I took very seriously. Every day I had another person to look after and think about, mainly because we shared a room together, but also over time, we developed that sisterly bond thing you hear about in sappy movies.

We were so close that I once saved her life from a fire, a story I did not let my parents forget for years to come. You know how you hear family stories over and over again, so much that they take on a very clear form in your mind, almost to the point where you remember it perfectly well, even though you were super young and probably didn't remember any of it? That's what happened with the fire story.

From what I recall, Caitlyn and I were hanging out by the couch, playing with our classic 80's toy collection of My Little Pony and Teenage Mutant Ninja Turtles, when my mom explained that the dryer was on fire. Now, what I'm sure happened in reality was that my mom told us to stand by the back door, ran to the fire extinguisher she intelligently kept in a well-known space and ran to heroically save the house from burning down by extinguishing the fire. However, in my five-year-old mind, I was the one who saved the day. I took Caitlyn to the back door, carrying her fireman style over my shoulders. This was a feat in itself because she had a good fifty pounds of baby weight still on her, and I broke through the glass pane of the door, tumbling out just as an explosive burst of flames reached out to grab us. You can believe whatever story you want to, but I'm pretty sure my version is closer to what happened. And I didn't even get a real pony for my bravery. Whatever.

This rebuff of rewarding the older sister is what might have caused me to do nothing when Caitlyn almost got killed by the dresser. This is known in my family as 'the time that big dresser fell on Caitlyn' and as I type it out, I am laughing uncontrollably at the sights and sounds from that day.

Caitlyn and I shared a room for most of our adolescence even though there was a perfectly good room right next to it that was used for toys. It could have had plenty of space for a twin bed, but I think my parents shoved us in together to bond or look out for each other, neither of which happened as evidenced by this story. In our room, we had an old wooden dresser that stood about four feet high. Today I could lift it on my own with ease, but as a child it stood massively high above us, holding all our days of the week underwear, skorts, and more screen printed t-shirts with images of Barney the dinosaur, Winnie the Pooh, and Looney Toons characters than you could imagine.

One of the things my mom is well known for is scouring the alleys for furniture. Which would be fine if it weren't for the fact that she read *The Velveteen Rabbit* to us as children; a story about a toy rabbit that gets thrown out because his child owner contracts some disease where all of his belongings have to be thrown out because they are covered in germs. If you ever want to become a germaphobe, read *The Velveteen Rabbit*. This book causes me to run for the bleach whenever my mom brings home a new treasure from the alley. I won't mock her too much though, because she has found some great pieces, including the dresser. A quick slab of pastel pink paint and some heart stencils, and it was like a new dresser- only the drawers would stick a little from the paint, which is how Caitlyn almost died. (I'm not painting a very nice picture of my mother here, and I apologize. Sorry mom, at least I saved Caitlyn from that fire for you.)

Caitlyn at the time of this tale was whatever age you are when you are three feet tall. The internet says four so we'll go with that. We were getting ready to go somewhere that required putting on clean clothes, so Caitlyn reached for a top drawer to grab a clean pair of underwear. But the drawer stuck, and because she was too short to hold the top part of the dresser down while jiggling the drawer open, she pulled the dresser ON her.

What happened next was a symphony of hilarious sounds. First there was the shrill shriek of terror from my sister, who was about to be crushed by the very thing that housed her Baby Bop (Barney the dinosaur's younger sister) frilly bottomed sweatshirt. Then there was the yell of my mom, who materialized out of nowhere at the sound of one of her children in despair (see- she's not just a dumpster-diving crazy lady), which sounded like wooouuaAHHHHH OH MY GOD! And finally, the growing cries of my sister, who wasn't really injured, but more frightened by the concept that a big pink dresser tried to end her. This might be why she went through a black-clothes phase in high school. Actually, she still doesn't like pink. I think I just pinpointed the source of my sister's inner angst. Hilarious!

What is troublesome I guess is that I didn't help her out really. I was paralyzed with shock when it all went down, unlike my fire saving incident. But, and mainly because she wasn't harmed, it turned out for the best that I was able to take it all in because that is one of the funniest moments in my sister's life that I can tell her for years and years. Unlike the time I almost broke her and my neck, leaving us (nearly) paralyzed.

For some reason, after the dresser incident, my mother still entrusted me to hang out with Caitlyn on our own while she was off doing things like battling fires or salvaging treasures from alleys. I kid of course;

she was probably making a nutritious meal for us, awaiting my dad to get home from work. (Is that a good enough Norman Rockwell description for you mom? Either way, I'm going to hear about this as soon as it is read, so I'll go on.)

In 1996, the summer and winter Olympics were a huge deal. I have a friend that makes fun of the U.S. for not getting more pumped about the Olympics as much as the rest of the world. What she doesn't understand that it's pretty difficult to top the drama that surrounded the 1996 summer Olympics, where the Magnificent Seven women's gymnastics team dominated the gymnast floor, and Kerri Strug, that tiny little girl, stuck the landing, even though she hurt her foot! Ugh, I am getting choked up just thinking about all the emotions! And not to mention, the crazy, twisted tale of Nancy Kerrigan, who merely weeks before the Winter Olympics was clubbed in the knee, which linked back to fellow Olympic ice skater Tonya Harding. Oh, the scandal! This all led to Caitlyn and I becoming entranced with the world of gymnastics, which then led to us almost dying in a tumbling-related accident that no one could have prevented. (Perhaps).

On this particular day, we were playing tumbling, which was variations of me trying to balance Caitlyn, a forty-some pound five-year-old on my weak nine-year-old legs and arms. All tumbling activities would happen in my parents' room because it had the most amount of space. Like I said before, we were privileged to have an entire room full of toys and games for our entertainment right next to our room, yet that was no match for the king-sized mattress and TV set up in my parents' room. Their bedroom served as a padded wrestling ring, tumbling mat, and nap zone for Caitlyn and me.

For months, we attempted the infamous toss, where I envisioned Caitlyn balancing on my feet and hands while I sat like a dead stiff animal with my legs and arms in the air below. She would lock her hands with mine, match her tiny feet to my large nine-year-old hooves, and once we were in position, I would push off into the air, where she would do a somersault in midair and land on her feet next to me. Unfortunately, I had no muscle mass, and Caitlyn was not Kerri Strug, so we never even got through step one.

Instead, we moved on to something we both thought would be easier- sitting on my shoulders while I walk around the room. I had seen my dad do it a bunch of times with her and figured it was easy. We started out slow, I was sitting on the bed with my feet hanging off, and Caitlyn sat on top of my neck, her short legs hanging over my shoulders. That alone was difficult and took a few tries before we got it down. When I thought we were in good form, I stood up from the bed, only to have her massively heavy body wobble around above me as I tried to maintain my balance. I instantly knew that it wasn't going to work and tried my best to toss her back onto the soft bed, but it happened too fast. I remember seeing a sock in my face as she kicked me on the way down, just as I heard a sharp CRACK sound coming from my neck, and we both tumbled to the floor.

In three seconds, my entire life flashed before my eyes. I knew we were paralyzed, I just knew it. My mom would find us after screaming up the stairs for us to eat dinner, and only after the third time, she would come to find our twisted bodies, wriggling on the ground like a bunch of fish on land. I would be in SO much trouble for paralyzing my sister; I wouldn't get to play outside with my friends all summer long, if ever. My dad would probably never let me have ice cream ever again, and we'd probably have to sell the king-sized mattress since we would need wheelchairs and gauzes for our heads that suffered rug burn from landing on the carpet.

Then I heard something even more terrifying than my neck cracking- it was Caitlyn starting to cry.

She started out with a low whimper as if to say, hey I'm still alive over here, why aren't you helping me? Then it grew louder, into a loud, long start of a wail. I flung my injured body over to her, clasping her mouth shut with my hand. She looked at me with the betrayal of an Olympic ice skater who got clubbed by her teammate. I was the Tonya Harding to Caitlyn's innocent Nancy Kerrigan, and I single-handedly ruined her career in balancing on people's shoulders for life.

'SSSHHHHHH.' I yell-whispered, hoping to negotiate with her. Even though I was the oldest and clearly to blame, we were both warned several times before not to jump off the bed. In fact, I'm pretty sure there is a song involving monkeys jumping off a bed that my dad sang to us on several occasions. If only we had listened. Even though this was not technically the same as jumping off the bed, the results were similar, and while I would surely get the harsher punishment and the rickety wheelchair, I said the one thing that can quiet even the most badly injured five-year-old. 'Mom will hear you.'

Caitlyn's eyes widened, her mouth gross and slobbering out tears that were being caught by my hand, but she immediately shut up. We both lied there on the maroon rug, quietly whimpering to each other, sad that we would never be able to move again, waiting for our mother to find us and carry our bodies to the hospital.

Luckily, we were fine. About five minutes later I tested out my limbs and found that Caitlyn did not, in fact, snap my neck in half. I helped her up too, and though she probably still doesn't completely trust me, we bonded over the mutual fear of almost breaking our necks and getting yelled at by mom.

I think the best revenge Caitlyn got on me was being four years younger and cute when I was going through my awkward phase. After my mom stopped worrying that Caitlyn was a preemie and would be a small kid, thus over-feeding her, Caitlyn thinned out and became an adorable looking kid. I knew something was a foul when people would come over to visit and gushed over what beautiful daughters my parents had, but only really looked at Caitlyn while I tap danced in the background.

As an ugly man-faced eleven-year-old with baby fat, big feet, and a penchant for horrible short bowl haircuts, the last thing anyone needs standing next to you is a cute as a button seven-year-old. As the hormones in my body were morphing me into a she-beast, my sister looked like a kid that you would find in a commercial for Sunny D, adorable and sweet looking, with a big heap of lovable. I did not survive puberty very well, but I don't think anyone does. Still, it was nice to have a little sister around to hang out with when your friends were being mean, or when you couldn't go out and wreak havoc on the night because your parents wouldn't let you stay out past dark. Mostly though I just screamed at her to bring me something to eat from the fridge, which she obliged, sometimes.

After I saved her once, let her almost get crushed once, and nearly broke her neck, my sister and I drifted apart. It wasn't anything dramatic, which kind of sucks for me because when you are writing a book about your life, it's much easier when there are big dramatic scenes you can use. But we just had our own thing going on. I think my parents planned it out well in having us four years apart. Both of my parents had siblings a lot older or younger than them, but having us four years separate was perfect. My mom always says it was well planned that she didn't have two kids in college at the same time, which was genius. But also it was nice to have the high school experience on my own, and I'm sure Caitlyn was glad I wasn't roaming the halls looking to shove her into a locker or join the tumbling team with me. (There was no tumbling team in our high school, although I would have started one if we were closer in age.) Caitlyn had her friends, and I had mine. Then I went on to college but lived at home so she could still be close to me, even if it was just sleeping in the next room and getting me a bucket while I was passed out from a college party. It's the little things, you know?

Then we hit our twenties, and everything shifted back around. Caitlyn was no longer that cute little kid or that big weird kid. She wasn't a kid at all. And it took me thirty years to figure out that she grew up a little bit, which I still ignore sometimes. She was the maid of honor at my wedding, and when I asked her she was a little surprised, which made me realize we weren't that close. But a year of me crying to her that I couldn't find the perfect shade of peacock blue to dye my shoes, and we went right back to being best friends.

I am not a manager yet in my profession, but I think it is a good sign when the people who work for you can not only figure out their own problems, but will go above and beyond to help you with yours. I still try and tell Caitlyn what to do, but for the most part, she's got it taken care of. Whatever she does with her life, she is going to be awesome at it and will have loads of fun doing it. That being said, I'd like to write a letter of recommendation to any future managers that might be interested in hiring my sister to work for them.

Dear Hiring Managers:

It is with great enthusiasm that I write this letter of recommendation for my sister, Caitlyn. As her older sister, I have come to know her quite well and can attest to her work ethic in great detail. Whether it is doing a load of laundry for my mom, even though it was technically my turn and she already did the dishes last time, or driving me home from the bar when I call her at two in the morning hammered, she is always there to get the work done, and never complains.

I am jealous of the coworkers that will get to spend their work week with my sister. While she is an incredibly hard worker, she is also a lot of fun. She would bring life and entertainment into any workplace, as evidenced by the days' long car trips to Florida that would have been nightmarish if it weren't for her eagerness to play car games.

Whatever she does, she's going to go far. Just so long as she watches out for those falling dressers.

Sincerely,

Caitlyn's big sister

The Story of Box Mountain and Best Friends

WORKING WITH YOUR BEST FRIEND is the best. If I didn't have such a weak stomach for blood, I'd have followed Alicia (That's Ah-LEE-see-ya, Not A-Lish-a. Please don't read her name wrong in your head- that would bug me this entire chapter.) on to become an ER nurse where we'd have the *best* time pretty much recreating the show *Scrubs* except without all the emotional scenes. It would include us making fun of patients and me getting hit in the eye a lot.

I met Alicia in kindergarten, and we became super close best friends in middle school. Most of my weekends in grades 7-12 were spent sleeping on her couch. We would wake up to the sounds of her grandma, the greatest grandma ever, working through her household chores of laundry, dishes, or making a pot of Guatemalan black beans. Important: If you are ever on death row and can't think of a last meal to request, ask for Alicia's grandma's black beans. Maybe with a little sour cream and some white sandwich bread.

Trust me; you will not be disappointed. Well, maybe a little with the whole death row thing, but not with the beans. They are God sent as is Alicia's grandma.

My best friend is a knockout! She has light brown skin from her Central American born parents, thick black hair that she used to wear long but now she wears her hair short which is so frustrating. If I had gorgeous black shiny hair and knew how to maintain it like she does, I would grow it out super long. But I guess it's hard maintaining gorgeous locks all the time. I wouldn't know. Whatever. I'm not jealous you're jealous. She's also shorter than me and petite, so when we stand next to each other, I can see over her pretty hair and if I'm in heels her head's closer to my shoulders. In fact, most of my closest friends are short. My wedding photos look like I'm friends with a bunch of children because they're all short, petite and young looking. I need uglier, taller friends!

Alicia always had this influence over me where she could simultaneously keep me level headed and safe while at the same time inspire me to do some of the dumbest, craziest things in my life. Past examples include giving myself bangs right before freshman year pictures, wearing an Aerosmith t-shirt and gym shoes to our junior prom over my dress. (I went to high school in the 2000s, not the 70s. But they just came out with their *Just Push Play* album, and I was getting into classic rock because the dude I was seeing was into all that. So if you look at my junior prom photos, you'll see me dressed randomly looking like a 1970s rock chick while everyone is in nice formal attire. Whatever, at least I didn't get knocked up.)

It's extremely difficult right now to restrain myself from writing nine million inside jokes that only her and I would understand. So while I'm reminiscing about random phrases like "light your shoes on fire!" and "Sideburns needs to shave herself" feel free to think of how awesome your own best friend is and when you've established a character connection, go ahead and move on to the next paragraph. If you don't have a best friend, just know that when I die I want her buried with me, even if she's alive, like those Egyptian pharaohs used to do with their slaves to keep them company in the afterlife. Best friends FOREVER!

Alicia was the one to convince me to attend our high school, Mother Guerin, which was a small all-girls school on the northwest side of Chicago. (Nowadays the school is co-ed and allows boys inside. I feel bad for the girls who go there now and can't look like gross slobs and act like lunatics without boys nearby.) At first, I was considering another Catholic high school, St. Ignatius, which had things like chandeliers, big libraries, and fancy carpets in the hallways (and boys!). I would have been just like Rory Gilmore attending Chilton, but I couldn't leave my Lane behind, plus it was really far, almost downtown, so I followed Alicia to Guerin. It's cool, Guerin had a library too. In fact, we spent a lot of our time in school there. See, when you go to a same-sex school that doesn't allow off-campus lunch and your boyfriend doesn't go to the all-boys school next door, the only real sense of freedom is getting a pass to the library. Sure you could sit in a quiet classroom for study hall, but who wants to do that when you can go to the library! Need to research that American government project that's due in two months? Sure! Leave my lecture and go to the library!

What harm can happen there? I'll tell you what harm-you can end up finding porn on the internet.

We were sitting at the computers in the library one day, which were right across from the librarian's desk when you entered the room. This was well before the days when kids knew that anything cool was on the internet, and Myspace hadn't even reached our age demographic yet. The only things we knew that were on the internet were research and porn. Bored, which let's face it, is 50% of the motivation teenage girls do anything in high school, the other 50% being boys, we decided to cruise the 'net. Being a Catholic school and all, the computers were heavily blocked, not just by the librarian standing fifty feet away, but also by website-blocking software that was supposed to be foolproof against reckless teens. We decided to hack into various fun websites for a while to see if it was possible to get into anything non-school related, and by 'hack' of course I mean we typed in 'AOL' and the 'website blocked' warning came on. Then, we typed in 'porn' and for some reason a million images of naked people popped up on the screen. I tried clicking out of them but the computer froze and we ran away. Thank GOD the librarian was not at her desk, or we would have been suspended and I would have to tell my mother and father I was caught looking at porn on the internet which would have ensured my spot in a pew every Sunday until I was thirty.

The last story from the Guerin library is less filthy. The internet had advanced a lot since the two years prior. Either that or the school put internet coding into the curriculum since the viewership on porn was skyrocketing at the school. So in our advanced placement English class, not only did we have to read a short story, but we also had to make a webpage detailing the author's biography and story elements. This was in 2002 so don't give me that crap about how easy it is to make a website. It wasn't that easy back then. You couldn't just download Google's latest blogging service (Did Google even exist in 2002? I don't remember. We used Ask Jeeves, and he didn't know a lot.) We had to use something called Microsoft FrontPage, and it was extremely tricky, especially if you were a teamed up with a crazy person, which Alicia was, and I was that crazy person.

I was struggling in AP English my senior year. I had fought my way into the class and was breaking my back earning grades not worthy of being put on a fridge. That is, until we read *Catcher in the Rye*. Having read the book in 7th grade when my mom gave it to me, hoping it would relate to the angst building up in her once cute daughter, I was in love with Salinger and finally got my first A in the class. So when the chance came to pick our own story to read, I pleaded with Alicia to make a J.D. Salinger webpage with me, hoping that our teacher, Ms. Tesauro, would remember my fleeting brilliance. The only problem was that Alicia and I are overachievers, which was proven in freshman year when we had to write out a diary creating a story of fictitious characters during the Holocaust. It would have been fine to each write one on our own, but being the grade whores that we were, we decided to combine our storylines and cross-narrate them in each of our diaries. It was just like when Ben Affleck and Matt Damon wrote Good Will Hunting, except they weren't being graded on it, so theirs didn't really matter.

Back to Salinger. So there's this wonderful short story in Salinger's *Nine Stories* called *A Perfect Day for Bananafish*. It's sad and interesting and has a brilliant metaphor where the main character talks about bananafish. In my head, these were fish with bananas as fins. And if it meant spending the rest of our lives in the Guerin library, we were going to have swimming bananafish gifs that you could click on our website.

This was beyond both the technology and capability of both Alicia and I, so we enlisted the help of the computer teacher (yes there was only one) who worked with us for weeks to get those fish to fly. J.D. Salinger himself did not spend as much time on his career as we put into that ridiculous webpage, but by the end of the day there were clickable bananafish, and we were IMMORTAL. (This webpage no longer exists, unfortunately).

Even though I could have been the Rory Gilmore of Chicago, it was worth my sanity and entertainment to go to high school with my best friend. Oh, also she helped me meet the guy I married by making me go to a high school homecoming, but still, the porn thing was also worth mentioning because it is one of my favorite stories.

The longevity of our friendship can be highlighted by the progression of modern technology, specifically in ways of communication. When we were in grammar school, we'd call each other on the telephone. I, typically on the house rotary phone which we didn't get rid of until they changed some of the Chicago area codes from 312 to 773 and we'd have to dial three extra numbers which altogether took about 20 minutes on the phone's spinning wheel. Nowadays I marvel at how difficult it must have been to reach people on a landline, but I was young then and only went to school and jazz dance class, so the chances of reaching me at home were pretty high.

Things could have gotten touchy once we entered high school and had more of a social life, but we were able to stay connected for a few reasons. First, we went to the same high school and spent the majority of the day together. And second, we had pagers for the moments we were apart. Pagers were huge in the late 90s-early 2000s. Everyone says pagers were for drug dealers or doctors, but we were neither. Instead, we were teenage girls who needed constant contact with friends that came in a cute colored box that you could clip into your uniform, but you could only activate by finding a landline. And when you received a message it would either be a number to call back, or tons of cryptic messages like 143 (the count of letters in each word for 'I love you') 07734 ('hello' upside down) or if you're short for time, 14 ('hi' upside down). Makes no sense I know, but neither did most of the things we did in high school.

Having social lives and pagers meant we had more of a need for cash, so when Alicia started working in high school, my afternoon entertainment plummeted. Luckily she was able to get me a job where she worked. AAA Furniture was an antique furniture store close enough for us to stop at her house for some afternoon beans from her grandma before heading in for our afternoon shift. It was like we were salesmen in the 1950s stopping home for lunch, only we would change out of our high school plaid uniform skirts and into our work clothes (sweatpants and hoodies), watch some TV and head down the street.

AAA Furniture was a family owned antique shop run by a family of smokers. There was Sam the dad, a big jolly type that probably was recruited by his family at one point to play Santa, which probably worked well since he was jolly and smelled like a chimney. Peggy, his daughter, was our boss and had a cool older sibling vibe since she was a freshman in college. Sam Jr. was also running around doing things with a cigarette hanging out of his mouth. Alicia and I were the outsiders, as were the truck drivers and salespeople. But working with a family is one of the best setups you can find in an employer because if you are working for a family and they haven't killed each other over money, chances are it is a very calm and friendly work environment. Why do you think mob families last so long? Deep down, they love each other to pieces. Luckily, the Smokers family let us into their work-home to earn some cash after school. But although they were a joy to work for, I imagine the reverse opinion wasn't the same. Imagine being trapped in a room with two teenage girls who've known each other for life. Between the inside jokes and obsession with boys, we were probably an employer's worst nightmare.

Our job was as follows- take pictures of all the antiques in the store that were decent and pack them up once they sold on eBay. You would think this would be a simple task, but you'd be wrong. Dead wrong! I'm surprised at how ridiculously banged up I got from what should have been a simple after-school gig. To this day I proceed with caution when handling X-Acto knives and packing tape guns because after weekly cuts and scrapes I realized those items are tools, not toys.

On one particular day, possibly over-caffeinated by Thai coffee that we would always get from the restaurant next door, Alicia and I were particularly restless. Peggy at the time was taking college night classes, and we were often left to our own devices. The first self-declared task of the day was getting a particular empty box that was the perfect shape for a silk lampshade we were shipping. The problem, however, was that this perfect box sat atop what we called Box Mountain in the large storage supply room. In reality, it might not have been as high, but my imagination has made me recall that box mountain was a good thirty feet tall.

We spent the first half hour of the workday arguing who would be the one to climb Box Mountain. I lost because, well honestly because Alicia was the bossy one and I was the comedic sidekick. I'm not complaining- this setup worked well for us and I was happy to have served as the Milhouse Van Houten to her Bart Simpson.

We sized up the mountain and determined the best course for me to take- using the smaller boxes as leverage since they were less likely to collapse than the bigger, more flimsy ones. Since she didn't want me to die (just get hurt a little) we cleared out all the sharp and breakable items nearby so that when I fell, it would just be on the concrete floor. By this time I was a little nervous, not having prepped for breathing in heightened elevation, but was determined to get that perfect box, and proceeded to trek uphill.

About halfway up, I could see clear over into the nearby suburbs. Frightened of the chance of stepping on a wobbly box, I moved a step every 5 minutes, while Alicia screamed "goooo" like a mountain goat from below, throwing empty tape rolls at me to move the process along. Then, as I neared the summit, I was overly excited to grab my treasure that I leaped towards the box, clenching it as I rolled down the hill, scraping myself on boulders of empty box flaps along the way. While I managed to ruin 90% of Box Mountain in my quest, climbing my Everest and grabbing the lampshade box was one of the single greatest accomplishments of my work history to date.

By this time half the day was gone, but we still needed packing peanuts. Typically, we would flirt with the drivers to get us a few of the four feet tall filled bags from the basement, but everyone was on a pickup run, so once again it was up to us. The problem though was that the basement of the store was about 3,000 square feet, and with the lights off, it was a perfect set up to be murderized to death by oh, I don't know, a creepy serial killer who wandered in the back door and waited for two beautiful high school girls to be distracted by a lampshade box to sneak in and wait to kill us? Or even worse- there could be mice! Whatever was down there, it wasn't safe enough for one man to go alone, so I convinced the convincer to go with me as we traveled down into the abyss.

Equipped with nothing but our faith in God, we crept down the creepy staircase. Pressed against the wall, we were feeling it up for lights, only to have to stop to shriek every half step as we touched another spider web. At one point, we decided it would be less scary to simply close our eyes, walking down completely blind to whatever was waiting to kill us. Upon reaching the light switch, we flipped that sucker on, only to find a bag of packing peanuts staring us in the face, and behind it was one large, creepy ass room filled with furniture your great-grandmother probably sat on. Hearing the killer upon us (or perhaps a customer upstairs walking on a loose floorboard) we grabbed the bounty and high tailed it out of there, screaming the entire flight up. Reaching the safety of the back room, we shut the door on the imaginary killer only to be face to face with Peggy.

Half attempting to explain our productivity in the day while gasping for air, I kept pointing at the box and peanuts, as if to say "Look! We got stuff done! I don't know why it is 7 o'clock and none of the items are packed!" But between the screaming, laughing and crying to the point we could not breathe, and the sound of more boxes falling down Box Mountain cliff, it was clear what our fate was- after winter break I got an awkward call from Peggy explaining that they were cutting back hours, and that since Alicia was the first hired, I was cut from the fun of box climbing and peanut packing. Bummer.

After graduating high school, it was my turn to pick the school. I was set on DePaul University in the city, and she had a scholarship that would make going anywhere else seem crazy, so it wasn't too hard to convince her. It sucked though because my classes were mainly downtown and she was in the Lincoln Park campus further north in the city, so we barely saw each other, except for the weekends. We didn't attend too many school-related functions, but one time our friend Norma took us to this huge house party near the Lincoln Park campus and we all got HAMMERED off of jungle juice. (You might call it something else depending on where you live- but it was a delightful concoction of Everclear, whatever hard alcohol was lying around, and Kool-Aid.) Alicia, being about half the weight I am, almost died off of one cup, which didn't have so much Kool-Aid as it did Everclear. But the party was still kind of fun and had good music. Yay college!

You would think, like many relationships, that we would eventually drift apart and lose touch, only sending Christmas cards and occasional likes of Facebook posts through the years. Nope. I was promoted to maid of honor and speech giver for her wedding. That came with the impossible task of throwing my perfectionist best friend a bridal shower and bachelorette party.

Honestly, if given the choice of planning parties or trying meth, I think I'd go for the meth. How bad can it be? Jesse from *Breaking Bad* seemed to enjoy it. Whatever. I probably would not choose harsh drugs over selecting shower invitations, but the stress of picking out the right centerpieces and matching desserts nearly sent me into an early grave. Now I understand why parents get so crazy when their kids' big day comes- you want everything perfect for your little one, no matter who you have to murderize to get it. Whatever. I am not good with the details, just the big picture stuff. Which is why my speech kicked ass.

I wrote my speech at four in the morning one night after reading an email Alicia had sent earlier in the night about what kind of drinks we should serve at the shower. I was annoyed that she had thought that I wouldn't know what to order to drink (so, no on the jungle juice then?). I'VE BEEN DRINKING WITH YOU MY WHOLE LIFE, I KNOW YOU LIKE SANGRIA, ALICIA. And from that, I couldn't sleep. And since I couldn't sleep, I decided to not waste any more time and opened my laptop and wrote the most beautiful speech ever. That's what friendship is- being irrationally pissed yet writing a beautiful speech about how much you love them.

It was a summary of this entire chapter. It was hard compacting twenty-five years of friendship, but somehow I managed to summarize everything into the cliff notes version pretty well. I kept having to go over it and make sure it was about her NEW best friend, her husband, instead of OUR friendship, but there was still so much I could have added. Like how she's always there for me when I'm pissed off and need to vent. Or how we are hilarious together and can make each other laugh at the most ridiculous stuff, like Tina Fey and Amy Poehler, but way funnier.

Anyway, I could go on and on, but it's time for the next chapter. Despite being grownups now with important jobs (Well, hers is important in that she can help save lives in the ER, mine is important in the sense that I know how to use an Excel pivot table, but more on that later.) we still Google chat each other every day. The other day we were both distracting each other- she was studying for yet another certification, and I was trying to edit this book. I think that's the best way to realize who your best friend is- someone who you'd most like to goof off with when you should be doing your work.

The Ecosystem of a Family Friendly Restaurant

WORKING IN A RESTAURANT is one of the most difficult jobs you can ever have. Okay, I should probably take out jobs that put your life on the line, or require holding a gun, or dealing with wild animals, and probably some other occupations that involve toxic chemicals...

Let me start again.

Working in a restaurant is one of the most difficult jobs you can ever have where there is a real concern you will be eaten alive by a hungry table of six. It takes quick thinking, an outgoing personality, and loads of inner strength to not swear at a customer. In fact, hostessing should be required for all applicants of any high-powered jobs. If you are able to successfully seat a group of 20 in a packed restaurant without crying, you, my friend, are CEO material.

Taking care of a customer in a restaurant is similar to dealing with a fussy baby. They are loud, need to be fed instantly before they have a meltdown, constantly need attention, drool, and sometimes vomit when they've had too much to drink. The invention of the word 'hangry' is the best adjective ever formed to describe the angered rage customers have when fueled by hunger, which is how most people enter a restaurant. Whether you are dining at a five star establishment or pulling up to the drive-thru, chances are you are ready to snap with a hunger-induced rage at a moment's notice, and the person serving you is the only one standing in your way from the deep friend antidote.

After the furniture store, I had another friend hook me up with a job working at a pizza place called Luigi's. It was on the northwest side of Chicago and nowhere near my house or school, making me a master at speeding down side streets, and other tricks such as learning to blow dry my hair with the car heater on blast. I started out as a hostess, but was eventually sent to the dungeon, aka the phone room, which suited me nicely since I have a low tolerance for dealing with the public. See, customers typically don't like it when you are waving your middle finger at them while they demand a booth during the dinner rush. But when they are asking for a cheese-free pizza over the phone- it's fair game.

The phone room was also great because it allowed me to see the whole inner workings of the restaurant operation, all while sitting in a comfy, pizza stained chair.

Red-Light Hostess Section

Did you ever notice that they put the pretty, innocent looking girls in the hostess section? No?

That's probably because your hostess was busy distracting you with her wide-eyed doe look and pretty curls long enough for you to forget that you have been waiting for a seat ever since you hit puberty. Good restaurants place the pretty, non-threatening looking girls at the hostess stand for two reasons:

1. To distract you from your stomach growling by making you happy to be near a nice, pretty, bubbly person.

2. To make you less likely to start an argument about not having a table, because who could ever be angry at a girl with Disney princess eyes?

The inner workings of a hostess stand are actually much more complex than they appear. In my brief time up front, before the managers realized that I swore more than a drunken sailor and would be better suited with the other miscreants below deck, I got a glimpse at what it would be like working at De Wallen, Amsterdam's most popular red-light district. Just like a brothel, you are basically on stage, smiling, luring pizza-thirsty Neanderthals into your room long enough to take all their money and leave them only temporarily satisfied. Luigi's worked us from both angles because not only did we have to stand upright and look pleasant for waiting patrons, but the hostess stand was also placed directly next to the bar where local schlubs would hang out and gawk at the pretty high school girls while crying into their Miller Lites with a shot of vodka in them (or as I like to call it, the 'my life peaked in high school' cocktail).

Although we were put up on our pedestals for eye lurking and gawking delight, the restaurant was nice enough to require us to wear the least appealing uniforms on earth- black polo shirts with khakis. If you are ever in a situation where you need to find the most unflattering outfit in existence, try wearing a black polo shirt and khakis. Single friends, are you getting ready for a first date and afraid you'll take things too far? Just try wearing a polo shirt. Nothing kills the mood like the unbuttoning of three buttons on a shirt and having to stop- it's like your cock-blocking best friend is right in the room, nagging at you to make better choices! To this day I cannot bring myself to buy a pair of khakis without thinking of pick up orders and seating charts. They also make my butt look lumpy, so it is probably for the best anyway.

Despite the life of drunken lures and ill-fitting outfits, there is a lot of work that goes into the job of a hostess. They must be able to solve seating arrangement-based equations that are so complex, MIT math professors study them. It might sound like an easy task- take a group of four and seat them in a four-top. Problem solved!

Wrong. You are so wrong.

In reality, the group of four is coming in with no reservation at 7 PM on a Saturday night. They are loud, sassy women who are not above complaining to a manager in the first five minutes of arrival. You look at your seating chart and find that the only tables available are one high-top, which will not do well for this robust group, and it doesn't matter anyway because the waitress for that table said that she will cut you with a bread knife from the kitchen if she gets another seating of bitches in her section. One would think she is on her period, but that's just her sunny disposition. There is a

10-top open which you can break down into smaller tables, but your manager already said that you have to leave that table open in case the owner's forty-year-old son comes in again with his dodgeball team after their game. The bitchy ladies of leisure are now blocking the entire front entrance with their attitude so you have to think of a solution like now, before the other manager working walks by and can't get through to flirt with your coworker, who has somehow managed to make khaki pants look sexy which just proves that life isn't fair. The solution? Seat the women in the scary waitresses' table, but lie and distract her by saying the cute new waiter had been asking about her. She'll be so happy that she will then spread the love to the four women who will be perched like volleyballs on a flagpole sitting on high stools, but will get over it with free apps. Everyone wins! And you don't get shanked in the kitchen!

My time up front ended quickly, but I did manage to survive the Super Bowl of hostess events...which was the Super Bowl. That day I managed to cry in the bathroom only once, have a waitress throw a pen as if it were a ninja star because I sat kids in her section, and made the mistake of walking in front of a customer during a crucial play that the guy was clearly upset about missing since he reacted by smashing his beer glass on the table, then tossed the table and got kicked out. Guess who had to clean up the mess? As I swept up shards of glass and French fries, I prayed for a better job position, something that didn't involve angry customers and angrier managers, perhaps out of the public image where I could work on more meaningful work like international relations. Perhaps something as fun and as thrilling as-the phone room.

The Part of the Restaurant That You Never Get to See

Restaurant managers are like taking shots- if you have a lousy one, you're in for a rough night. There were three types of managers at Luigi's: The general manager/head honcho lady, three wait staff/hostess managers, and one delivery/take out manager. That doesn't even include the kitchen which is run by the head chef, so technically I guess there are four types. Just like when I take shots, I'm already getting confused and can't do simple addition.

Denise was the scariest person I had ever met in my life at that point. A large, blonde, 6 foot behemoth who wore pant suits but could have just as easily been wearing a football jersey. She never smiled, unless she just got finished devouring an employee and had just pooped them out, forcing them to clean up the bathroom stalls while they recovered. She was mean, had a short tolerance for incompetence, and didn't mess around. But what made her evil (and therefore free for me to rip apart with a clear conscious now that I am far, far away from her) was her interaction with her employees.

Like many women after, Denise had what I have come to experience as the angry female boss character- a woman who feels she needs to prove herself to the world as a leader by being mean. Now before any feminists burn this book in anger, sending me hate emails on how if Denise were a man, I would call her a strong leader. No, I would not. If Denise were a Dennis, I'd simply call him an asshole. And Lord knows there are enough male asshole bosses riddled with their own insecurities that cause them to lash out at an employee, or cut a new employee's hours for not kissing ass. But what I am talking about here is a subculture of female bosses who deep down are frightened little girls who never had great people skills because their fear of getting picked on led them to develop a thick skin and a reputation as the mean girl on the playground. These types of women don't know how to get shit done, and for some reason have formed the visual in their mind that in order to look like a strong leader, you have to yell and scare the crap out of everyone around you.

A telling sign of this type of boss is that their actions are always reactionary to their own bad decisions- *Why didn't you mop up the floor even though I told you to only focus on cleaning tables today? Why is there a forty-five minute wait even though I told half the staff to stay home today?* While on the outside I see an angry woman yelling, inside I see a young girl taller than the boys in her 3rd grade class, wanting to be loved.

But hell if I'm ever going to use the bathroom if she's in there.

Second in command to the General Manager were the floor managers. These are the managers in charge of certain sections- the bar, the delivery room, banging the wait staff. I should write a description of each person here, but they were pretty much all exactly the same- white, older 30s, probably raised in a nearby suburb who all graduated from some form of Main East/West/North/South high school depending on their zip code at the time. I didn't have too much interaction with these guys because I wasn't a waitress, nor did I wear makeup, leaving them no reason to find an excuse to come in and flirt with me, unlike my pretty friends who did not dry their hair using their car heater. But the one manager I will never forget is Steve.

It was a warm summer day in July when my coworker Jessica and I were in the phone room. Phone room staff people had the best setup because we had an AC unit, which was actually more for the computers not to overheat, but whatever. We would use our cold air power as leverage when the drivers acted like assholes and banned them from the room whenever we deemed necessary. Yes, you may have found a way to come to America and find gainful employment (for real-delivery drivers make fat cash if a restaurant is hopping), but dare to refuse a delivery that is in our delivery zone and you are exiled to the sweaty kitchen by a seventeen-year-old!

Every single driver was Russian, and we had so many that there were duplicates. In order of annoyance, there was Boris 1, Vladimir, Boris 2, Igor 1, Igor 2, and Yakov, the oldest driver in all of Chicago. They were all very strong willed, and wouldn't budge to help you, because it didn't involve getting paid. I respect that. They weren't there to make friends and help you sweep or to carry things; they were there to deliver food in order to earn tips. But at the same time, I thought they were the most annoying bunch crybabies I've ever worked with.

Anyway, Jessica and I were sitting in the room one hot summer day wearing long-sleeved t-shirts under our polo shirts because the AC was so high, when we started to notice an odor. At first we assumed it was one of the older Russians who didn't like to bathe, unlike the younger ones in their 20s who bathed exclusively in cologne. But as the day turned into the early dinner rush, we kept noticing the stench. Being the go-getter that I am, I decided to explore. Our 7 x 9 foot room was cramped with one desk along the wall, two chairs, two phones, two computers, an extra desk that had a broken leg, and boxes of delivery flyers that were to be folded when we weren't busy taking orders and smelling foul odors. I started crawling under the desk, slithering past Jessica's feet. I was impressed by her ability to take orders with a straight face as I took my chair and a broom, pretending to be the Crocodile Hunter, searching for the rare stench in the jungle. As I reached the land of the extra desk, the foul scent grew stronger. Dinner time now, the phones were ringing nonstop, which slowed down my search only slightly. As I rattled off the appetizers to a friendly mother trying to order her kids' dinner before the babysitter arrived, I found the smell. There, underneath five boxes of delivery flyers was a flattened, decomposing mouse releasing the foulest stench you could imagine.

Nice Mom in Need of a Night Out was still ordering as I mouthed a scream to Jessica. As soon as we both hung up, we screamed bloody murder, which resulted in the entire Russian delivery squad entering our phone room, only to run out in terror after seeing the mouse. The sight of five big, burly Russian men running scared from a flattened dead mouse is something that will stay with me forever. Are all Russians this timid? Probably not. But none of them were willing to go anywhere near the thing even though I secretly offered Jessica's phone number to Boris 2 in exchange for the deed.

Phones ringing, Russian men crying, we were trapped with the flyer-flattened mouse with nowhere to run. I ran out into the restaurant looking for help when I crossed paths with Steve, floor manager for the night. I babbled something like, "There's flattened Russians and pizza mice trying to ask out Jessica! Help!" He looked at me, pissed, and briskly walked past me, heading straight for the phone room. He walked in, not knowing fully what to expect, seeing Jessica standing on the desk taking an order, pointing to the crime scene. In one fell swoop Steve grabbed my broom/ship paddle and a handful of flyers, swept up the stank-ass mouse, and walked out the door. I have never been so in awe of a manger's quick thinking. Steve was the manager I aspired to be, minus the job requirement to pick up dead mice.

You may have noticed that in this entire section on the back part of the restaurant that I didn't mention the chefs and cooks. You know why? Because it's too hard to describe what they do without giving them the proper credit they deserve. Imagine ten of your friends come over, and you have to cook a delicious, well-plated meal immediately before they get angry and de-friend you. Now imagine doing that hundreds of times in a night while 100 more of your friends are calling asking you to make them a pizza. I can't do them justice, so I'll just say that if you are a chef or a cook of a restaurant, you have my admiration. And I'm not just saying that because you can spit in my food and I would never know. Although that does haunt me, a little.

Waiting for a Better Attitude

There are two types of people in this world: nice people and assholes. The same applies to the wait staff subculture. But the way a waitress acts to their table is often times the exact opposite of what they are like in real life. Normal, human servers are the ones least likely to have a temper hotter than the pizza oven. Middle of the road, they smile at you and are quick with a refill. They do not make a dessert selection seem like they are making a presentation of the Nobel peace prize, but your food is hot when they bring it out, which is nice.

Cranky servers are probably the most difficult to decipher, but I still maintain my theory of opposites when it comes to this group. Chances are, if you have a server who is in a generally pissy mood, it's because they are doing the most work out of the others. There are a lot of less-glamorous tasks that servers have to deal with other than stuffing your gullet with food (shocking, I know). They have to do things like fill ketchup bottles and sometimes bus tables. The bubbly ones can easily get out of it without having a manger catch on by radiating so much cheesy niceness you could make a family-sized pizza with what is coming out of their mouth. But the ones who aren't willing to sacrifice their sanity with an over-the-top serving performance are stuck with mind numbing tasks around the restaurant and therefore get pissy. So the next time a waiter or waitress pours your coffee without a smile that changes your view on life, remember that they might be dealing with some horseshit behind the scenes that would put you in a stinky mood yourself.

There is one type of server that will straight up put the fear of God in you if you get in their way. The Long Island Iced Teas (or LIITs for short)- a server that is overly sweet and enthusiastic to the point that they make you feel like the sun is coming out of your butt for ordering a 16-ounce margarita and are often the meanest creatures behind kitchen doors. I call them the LIITs because just like the drink, they seem sweet and innocent, but will knock you on your ass when you least expect it. Probably because they are using all of their kindness in the hopes that you will give them a hearty tip to cover their bar tab at the darker establishment across the street with less crap on the wall. But beware- behind closed kitchen push-through doors, I have seen these energetic beings physically rip the heads off of cooks and degrade an entire team of bus boys to the point of oblivion.

At Luigi's, the servers were 80% LIITs. These 'ladies' were some coked-out crazies that could afford fake nails and lowlights, but only spent half a semester at Wright community college before they needed to take a break from studying to focus on more important things- like being evil to the cooks and hostesses. I thought these older girls were super cool and intimidating- like that one friend's older sister you had when you were young who had a boyfriend with a car and would come home late past her curfew. I used to think the reason they were put on server duty instead of being banished to the phone room of hell was due to their good looks. How I mistook their beer-bloated faces and hung-over drunken eyes for pretty is beyond me, but then again they were the bubbly group, so they had a hold on everyone.

As pretty as I thought they were, they also scared the living crap out of me. Rumors spread of how one waitress once punched out a drunk girl at the dive bar next door for stealing her lighter. Another waitress had a claim to fame for having s-e-x in the restroom with frat guys. And almost all of them regularly dashed through the snow in a one-horse open sleigh, if you know what I mean. (Full disclosure: I am so naïve with any form of serious narcotics that I can't think of a good analogy here. I should go watch Scarface or Blow but I don't really enjoy drug movies. Did my made-up reference to cocaine work? I sure hope so.)

The lifestyle of the LIITs was way beyond my level of understanding, and had my mother caught wind of the types of people I was working with, she would find every one of their mothers' phone numbers and call them to let them know exactly what went on at the restaurant. In order to save my mom a night of rosary praying and phone calling, I kept a safe distance from them, and only poked my head out of my nook when needed.

But despite the drug use and scary college girls, the waitressing lifestyle was growing more and more appealing, especially when I figured out how much they took home. Do you know how expensive coke is?? Waitresses, at least the ones in a popular restaurant that know how to entertain a table, make BANK. That's probably the part I was most envious about- we both left past midnight, equally tired and stressed, yet they walked out with at least quadruple of what I was making- in cash.

It didn't seem fair. I was taking AP English! I finished Charles freaking Dickens the same night I crammed for an Algebra II midterm! I didn't snort things up my nose! The world didn't make sense. My admiration grew as my curfew-trodden self would watch them hang out after hours in the bar getting free shots or wandering next door to Muller's, the bar located above a bowling alley, which I thought was the *coolest* bar in all of Chicago. I longed for the day when one of the LIITs would ask me if I wanted to join them after work. In my mind, I'd down jaeger bombs with them and keep an eye out in the bathroom while they snorted half of their tips up their nose, ending the night in a round of dancing in halter tops! What else could a seventeen-year-old girl ever dream for?

Three years later I got my answer. With my fake ID in hand, 'Brenda Meyers' dragged her friend to Muller's ensuring her that it would be the most fun we've ever had. What I found though was a sad display of humanity. The dark, musty bar was apparently where Luigi's employees go to die. It was like looking at how hot dogs were made if you ever thought hot dogs were living the glamorous life. Hunched over at the bar were the same LIITs I had once admired, wasted beyond belief, looking disheveled in their vodka-soaked polos drinking beer. As we left, the one I remembered as being the second-prettiest of the group, tumbled down the stairs, swearing at two men offering to help her up. Her polo rolled up out of her khakis, revealing a butt crack and beer gut that resembled Dan Conner's.

After that I quickly got over the lavish lifestyle allure of waitressing and decided to hold out for salaried jobs that didn't rely on my brimming personality or ability to stay awake with anything harsher than a triple latte with no foam (FYI, that's not a drug reference. At least I don't think it is.).

Discounted Pajama Pants

GROWING UP CATHOLIC is awesome around Christmas time. There are four weeks of pretty candles, a calendar filled with chocolate, and baby Jesus is coming to command one of his saints to deliver presents to good little kids and adults who still love Christmas.

I'm guessing casual Christmas fans- people who weren't forced to sit in a pew for most of their childhood weekends- are enjoying the holiday life sans-Christian beliefs as well. And who could blame them? There's so much going on that it's a celebratory free-for-all from the day after Thanksgiving until it's time to head back to work/school and brag about all the awesome presents you got. The entire month is just the best.

After my first quarter of college at DePaul University, I was in need of some fast cash for Christmas presents. Instead of semesters at DePaul, they had three quarters- Fall, Winter and Spring. What was utterly awesome about this was that fall quarter ended the day before Thanksgiving and winter quarter started after New Year's, leaving six glorious weeks of hibernation. St. Vincent, the patron saint of the school, is one of my top favorite saints because of this sole fact. (Sidenote: If I ever become sainted, which, looking at my life, I totally should, I want to be the patron saint of naps. Who wouldn't want that saint as their favorite saint? I sure would. Look out John the Baptist- I'm beheading your #1 spot.) With my first classes of my college career out of the way, I had free time to do wild and crazy things like finding a seasonal job for the holidays, since my boyfriend at the time was busy at the frat house he recently joined and Christmas presents needed to be purchased. So off I went to the nearest mall in search of employment.

The Harlem and Irving Plaza, or the HIP if you live in the '606' zip code region is the mall in closest proximity to my house that wasn't skeezy (Brickyard) or super fancy (Old Orchard). Here's a fun fact- the city of Chicago has more neighborhoods than Lakeview and Wicker Park. It's gross when people who are new to Chicago think the only parts of the city are within a three-mile radius of the Loop. Where do you think we all live? In expensive-ass studios in Lincoln Park? No. Definitely no. The northwest side, which is the broadest term ever for the area not near downtown, includes my neighborhood and basically every neighborhood until you hit the suburb of Park Ridge. It's filled with things like trees, front yards, gang ways, and yes, malls. The HIP wasn't even that close to my house, in fact it was 8 miles west of my house, the same distance to downtown. Why I chose to travel west for employment, I'm not sure. Probably because there is more parking and things to do on the northwest side for a young girl, like going to the HIP.

I got a seasonal job at Discovery clothing in the morning so that I could still have time for my main passion of pizza order taking in the evening. Discovery, if you've never frequented, is a cheap clothing store for women. The store sold mostly clubbing outfits that you would see at places like Zero Gravity, the underage club where I definitely, never went after pre-gaming in the parking lot with Bacardi O and Sprite (hi mom, and any daughters I may raise in the future). They also had things like khakis and collared shirts, but that style only covered one small area, with a larger section of polyester thongs on the other side, better known as the UTI aisle (We often had a deal of 5 UTI's for the price of 3!).

My job description included two things: putting clothes on hangers and manning the fitting room. Both of these things were so awful that it made me wish I was back finding dead rodents in the dingy phone room. I realize the difficulty of conveying the awfulness of working as a person who hangs up clothes might not be illustrated that well, so here are some cinema movie sadnesses to put you in the proper setting:

- Bambi's mother getting shot
- Any part of the Green Mile
- The end of the Notebook (It was us!!!!)

Hanging up clothes all day was the worst. Everyone on earth can relate to this because everyone on earth has a pile of clothes crumpled in a pile that should have gone on a hanger and now need to be rewashed or ironed, which they won't so they just sit there. And do you know why everyone has this pile? Because putting clothes on hangers is the worst!

What's even more awful is running a fitting room. At 18, I did not feel as though had the real world experience that would have prepared me for the horrors seen in that tiny, 3 stall room.

The clothes Discovery ran from 0 to 13. The women buying clothes in Discovery ran from sizes 0-142. If I had the amount of perseverance and determination as some of those women did trying to fit their gut into a size L tank top, I would be the CEO of Coca Cola by now. Shopping tip for everyone: when you buy clothes, check the seams to make sure a wishful shopper wasn't trying to smash their hopes and dreams into your next purchase. From what I've seen, there's a good chance they have. But the most trouble I would get were from the skinnies. Plus sized women typically didn't bring in spectators to their personal struggles, and sulked off quietly leaving ten pairs of pants in the dressing room to be rehanged, covered in tears. (I speak from experience on this one. Dear Ann Taylor, would it kill you to carry a size 16 in your downtown store during one particular winter after a long holiday season of gingerbread lattes? You madam, are a smug little bitch.) But unlike the plus sized patrons, skinny people had options and choices on how a shirt fits, not whether they *can* fit into a shirt. Those crazies left my rooms looking like a tornado hit Chicago, and all that was left behind was a hooker's wardrobe.

After the first week I got the hang of it. I hung out near the racks by the fitting room so I could put clothes on hangers *while* helping people in the fitting room. A real go-getter I was. By the end of the first week though I was already sick of the only CD that was authorized to play- a Christmas CD on ecstasy featuring a Nelly

Furtado song that to this day makes me want to take a gun to my head. Nelly Furtado, if you're reading this, please know that I hate you.

On Sunday of the second week, I came in that morning to find a slender gentleman trying to peer up a mannequin's mini skirt. He was tall, but slightly bent over at the shoulders, showing signs of scoliosis and so much dandruff on his head that one shake of his head and the city would have to cancel school. This guy made Urkel look like a teen heartthrob, and made it clear with his fake converse shoes, light washed jeans, and his pleather Marvin the Martian faux suede sleeved jacket. His name was Mark, and he was the new morning shift manager, which simply meant he had the key to open the gate to the front of the store in the morning and could work the cash register. Other than that, his power was limited, which was known to everyone but him.

Mark's first week was a bit of a blur for him, and more than twice I had to remind him the weekly thong specials (5 UTIs for the price of 3!) and every single time he mentioned "thongs" he would sing it like Sisqo in "Thong Song."

Connie, do you know how much the laced THONG-THA-THONG THONG THONGS cost? Connie, are the G string THONG-THA-THONG THONG THONGS cheaper than the bikini strapped ones? Sisqo, if you are reading this, please know that I also hate you.

He was the type of coworker who also liked to "chit chat." Not talk, not develop an interesting conversation, but chit chat in that he did all the chitting and chatting, leaving me annoyed 99% of the time. In the short time I knew him I managed to learn his entire life story. He was born in New Jersey, not near the fun part, because his parents hated going to the shore. His parents divorced when he was 11 and his mother moved them to Joliet so they could rent a two flat with her sister. His best friend in high school was Nick because he was on the Chess team and he didn't care for what he called the "wannabes" because he and Nick were more intellectual (Read: the cool kids kicked his butt. A lot.). When Nick went off to U of I in Urbana Champaign, Mark went to Columbia College in Chicago to play with his band, which consisted of him on his guitar and his cousin whose dad sometimes let him use his drum set. He later dropped out and started working so he could get his own place. One time, (and I think this was the only time he had sex, the only detail about his life that he left out), he visited Nick at U of I and got a philosophy chick pregnant. She wanted nothing to do with him but had the baby, a girl, and moved up to Wisconsin. Mark was now working at Discovery so he could hire a lawyer to get custody rights of his now four-year-old daughter whose name I forget.

I responded to this by sharing with him that pumped up Christmas music gave me a headache. He wouldn't change the CD.

By week three Mark was fully trained and started thinking outside the fluorescent lit walls of Discovery. He had a plan to reshape retail forever by holding the first ever Discovery staff meeting which consisted of me, a group of three retail ladies a little older than me and so unfriendly looking they could make the Grinch himself weep, and Christina, the thirty-something woman who hired me in under 10 minutes because I could work weekends. Christina was the real store manager, but she let Mark play CEO that morning to tell us all how great of a job we were doing, and to fill us in on his new great marketing plan. Every Friday, we would be allowed to wear pajamas to work, provided that we purchase them from Discovery, which could be purchased with our fabulous employee discount of 10% off, not including clearance items. I was pumped because it meant that I now had a legitimate excuse to purchase the fleece button down pajamas with pictures of rubber ducks wearing shower caps that I had been eyeing ever since I started working there. Mark may have wasted my first fifteen minutes of work by thinking up an employee chant, but he won me back by allowing me to wear PJs. Christina seemed hesitant and quiet, and the Unfriendlies were busy looking too cool to be anywhere that played Nelly Furtado.

That Friday morning was exceptionally cold, so I was super excited to jump out of bed and get into my new pajamas. When I arrived, I first saw Mark looking even whiter than usual. Past him, I spotted the leader of the three Unfriendlies sporting a fuzzy pink tube top and pajama bottoms with pink army camouflage print. Next to her was the most sensibly dressed one, in a similar ensemble, but with a zip up hoodie as well. The shortest girl, Elga, I shit you not, wore a faux silk negligee and matching silk booty shorts. And boots. Because of course you want your feet to be warm in the middle of December.

Being stationed in the back, I was able to hear Christina chew out Mark for his lack of slut prevention. She kept asking him how this would look if the regional manager stopped in to check up on the store and what would the customers think of this obscure display. Oh honey, I will tell you how this looks, it looks like you hired one crazy girl from a mental hospital who ran away in ducky pajamas and then hired three strippers to fill in for your employees being out. But I was too busy sweating my ass off in my fleece pajamas to care.

Things just got worse from there. Mark was now fully trained in the cash register, in a manner of speaking. He constantly kept mis-ringing items and had a hard time keeping track of what pieces were on sale, which included about two thirds of the store. Each week more and more customers kept filing in and it broke out into a state of constant madness once the high schools were out on winter break. Mark couldn't keep control of his employees. I was a saint of course, only causing trouble on account of my constant lateness, a fault I still carry. I usually avoided get out of being docked any pay by distracting Mark and asking him what he thought we could do to improve the store layout. By the time he finished explaining his 35 point plan on total retail domination, it was time for lunch and he had forgotten about my late entry.

Every time Mark failed at the register or had a new promotional idea that failed miserably, his smugness grew, I suppose, to compensate for his shortcomings. By this time he was now one hand crafted pipe and a velvet robe away from taking the reign as being classified the smuggest bastard in the mall, second only to the Express clothing store sales associates. Those bitches were ten times cooler than us half-off sticker priced trash. But Mark tended to act as if he invented the word marketing even though each of his attempts at an in-store promotion led to more work and less revenue.

I tolerated his bullshit mildly, rolling my eyes hard core whenever he went to tend the register. But the Unfriendlies were less kind. The break time sign out sheet in the back room was graffitied with pictures of a mysterious "wizard" standing on mountains of thongs. Sometimes the wizard would be doing other things, like smelling the thongs, or once, wearing them. But the message was clear- Mark, er, the wizard, had no respect from his employees whatsoever. Even after he went through countless cavalier efforts that HR personnel have nightmares over, like buying the Unfriendlies Bacardi on the weekends since they were *only* two months away from turning 21 (more like two years), or driving them to the south side to pick up the main girl's boyfriend, who would blaze up in Mark's car as he dropped them off at the movies. Shockingly, none of these things made him more authoritative in the eyes of his employees, a case study that should be examined in the next Harvard Business Review.

Christina was taking more and more notice of what was going on as well. She started out by having daily catch up sessions with Mark, to see how things like inventory and customer wait time were going. Then she moved on to retraining him at the register, although when Mark described the process, it was 'managerial training to better understand best practices.' As things continued on, she even brought the girl who had worked there the longest to stand by him and point to the correct buttons when checking out large purchases. But no matter how many times he read the ten page manager instruction handbook, Mark just wasn't getting it.

Dante famously wrote about the 7 layers in hell. I didn't read it, but I'm pretty certain the 7th layer is working in a mall on Christmas Eve. Usually on this day, my father, sister and I are running around looking for that one item that my mom specifically asked for. One year it was a plain red button down cardigan. You would think that would be an easy find, but it took my dad and I six stores and a volleyball styled dive under the security gates into Carson's one year to find the damn thing. After a quick sprint around the women's department, my father came waving a red sweater over his head as if he was carrying the Olympic torch to the opening ceremonies, holding the thing high in the air with pride. If I ever find out my mom donated that cardigan, she's going in the old folks' home where they lie to them and say the TV is on when it isn't. But in all that hustle, I never bothered noticing how awful it was for the store employees who worked that night, which is why I was folding khakis on December 24th, 2003.

It was a shit storm. People were shoving, grabbing and pushing their way to grab that one last gift before it was time to close. I got shoved in the hips countless times with strollers and at one point a woman left me with her son so that she could carry all her belongings to the register. People of the earth, do not bring your small offspring to the mall with you on Christmas Eve, unless you want them to hate you and grow up to be a neurotic mess.

We opened at 6am and by 9am Mark had lost his mind. Customers were lined up down the aisles, past the puffy coats, through the jean racks, and clear out into the mall. Every purchase that he rang up was beeping the error message, to the point where Elga, who until this point showed no emotion, looked panic stricken. By 10:30am, customers were starting to get finicky, and it was getting out of control. At one point I considered hiding inside the circle clothes racks of pajamas, waiting for things to settle down, but was worried customers would start lighting clothes on fire, which would have burnt the place down in seconds with all the cheap fabric inside. Mark's voice grew higher and higher until he blew, like a kettle, and screamed, "Could everyone please come back in 15 minutes?" at which half the line threw down their items in unison and left.

Christina came in at noon even though she had the day off. I think one of the girls called her from the break room and told her about the situation which was probably the right thing to do considering the chaos that had been going on. Elga had to watch the register while Mark was called into the back. Unlike most of their meetings where I heard every word, things were extremely quiet this time. Minutes later, Mark came out, with his coat on and I asked if he was ok, but he walked quickly past me, red eyed and head down. He walked out of Discovery without a word, and the last image I saw of him was Marvin the Martian on the back of his jacket giving me the peace sign as he turned toward the exit. Nelly Furtado played loudly in the background.

Christina stayed the rest of the day and everyone else was working a double to earn overtime. I finished out the 14 hour day in a deep state of sad. Mark was annoying as hell, there was no denying that. And he was piss poor at his job for sure. But he came in every day with the enthusiasm of a five-year-old going to their first day of kindergarten, and I thought that should have counted for something. I felt sorry for him, and sorry for myself for working such a crappy job, wasting my entire break just so I could make a lousy $7 an hour over Christmas vacation. As I walked out the mall to my car, I was saddened by all the decorations mixed in with the lack of the holiday spirit. I felt dirty and cheated and kept thinking of Mark not getting to see his kid because he was fired on Christmas Eve. I vowed never to waste my precious holiday time, time I could have spent hanging out with friends or having dinner with my family, over a crappy seasonal job. And I never wanted to work for a person or company who only thought I was worth a 10% discount. I prayed that baby Jesus would smite down Discovery store and give Mark a second chance.

Somehow, this was all Nelly Furtado's fault.

File Bicycle Shorts Under 'S' for 'Smelly'

TOM PARKER WAS A stone cold fox. If it weren't for the fact that I was 40 years his junior, I'd be all over that. The HR manager of Long Distance Van Lines (LDVN), Tom was so smooth he made Don Draper look like a complete loser. Blue eyes, silver hair, and a smile that could sell a cheeseburger to a vegan- he had it all. At first when I thought this, I completely freaked out, thinking this sort of attraction is only reserved for people with high flying daddy issues. But a few years later my friend worked there for a summer and assured me that no no- he was an exception. A hot, old, charming exception.

I started working for Tom the spring of my freshman year in college. Through my first and only experience with nepotism, my mom's friend hooked it up with a part time job that was flexible enough for a young college student who liked to sleep off hangovers and do minimal amounts of work. I was the HR assistant for Tom, which has all the makings for one sexy porn movie, don't you think?

The other thing about Tom was that he was a man who needed no introduction. Because I couldn't give him one. Since he was way older than my nineteen-year-old self, I was too fearful to call him by his first name, since I was brought up to respect my elders (despite what you now may think of me). So instead, I would lurk in his doorway until he looked up so I could start speaking. Looking back, he probably took sympathy on me and thought that I must have some sort of lung disease with all the throat clearing I would do to get his attention. But in the 18 months that I worked for him at LDVN, I never once called him by his name. I was so proud of this accomplishment that I wanted to put it on my resume. I also want to put it on there because I didn't have much else to put under this job.

LDVN was located in a next door suburb of Chicago called Lincolnwood. The office was a three floor building tucked away behind a tree-lined cul-de-sac of really fancy houses that were too small to be mansions but too big to fit in the neighborhoods of the city. I would drive to work after school in my previously owned blue Toyota Corolla that my dad purchased the year after I was born. It was the perfect ride for anyone who didn't know how to navigate the suburban bus system, which is confusing. I worked after class on Tuesdays and Thursdays, and on Fridays I would work all day, unless of course a big exam was coming up. There were lots of exams that came up. And by exams I mean Thursday night Jager bomb specials. I studied a lot.

I started out in the HR office, which consisted of four cubicle spaces, stud muffin's office, and the Customer Service manager, who really had no business being there, except it evened out things so that there were two old men, two really old HR ladies, two thirty-something HR ladies, and myself. It was like Noah's ark with personnel. When I wasn't filing sensitive HR documents in the file room, I was stationed at a chair in between the four HR ladies. For five months I sat there, doing interpretive work, pretending for hours to be busy since Tom never gave me anything to do that took over twenty minutes to complete.

It always takes a while for me to scope out my coworkers and make allies. One of my winning personality traits is that I'm drop-dead quiet at first, only releasing my witty repartee to those whom I've deemed worthy of sharing it with. In the first month, I decided that Gladys, the first old lady, was not worthy. Gladys was about 970 years old, liked to eat oranges incredibly loud, and treated her work of logging data as if she was the president's personal surgeon and he'd just been shot. You would think the world ended every time her computer crashed, or a file was misplaced. She also had the perfect face to match her extreme nosiness, with a nose that poked out perfectly over the cubicle half walls. Her favorite hobby, as far as I could tell, included standing over my shoulder eating oranges while I worked on super public documents like W2 forms and job applications. My shoulders tightened in a permanent scrunch every time I was in that office.

Diane, the other old lady, hated the world, but was much more tolerable. Every single task resulted in a complaint. The phone's ringing? It's probably a dumb job applicant. The computer isn't working? It's probably because Gladys is an idiot. The thermostat is set to 71 instead of 70? Someone get me a gun to shoot myself with. To Diane, the world was her complaint box, and she always had it full.

To escape the chaos, I would hide in the barracks of a 4 foot by 6 foot room of filing cabinets where all the HR documents were stored, and I was in charge of filing them away. I could kill a good hour and a half with four folders and a concentrated face whenever someone would walk by. It was a nice break from the orange chewing noises, but looking back I basically sat in a prison cell of paper. Still, it was nice and peaceful at first, until the other old dude in the office started biking to work and my filing cabinet getaway turned into a stink hole of hell.

Guy Smith, which isn't his real name but conveys his blasé character appropriately, was not worth writing about. He wasn't outwardly mean, nor was he nice in any way. He wouldn't be in this book except that in the summer of 2005, Guy decided to bike the 22.4 miles to work every day, changing in the company gym locker room and leaving his sweat soaked shorts, shirt, and shoes in *my* filing room to air out before his ride home. The room that I would go to find solace and tranquility was now soaked in the sweat of a 22.4 mile bike ride. How did I know the distance that produced the sweat? I looked up his address in my filing room and mapquested it so I had a number to scream when I would tell the story to my friends after work. Looking up other people's personal information is pretty wrong and stuff, but you know what else is wrong? Making a perceivably hard working girl smell your junk sweat every day in a room smaller than a gas station bathroom. (For the record- it's also wrong to cut in front of said hard working girl in the lunchroom to use the only working microwave to heat up your Lean Cuisine.

Due to my chronic quietness, I endured the filing room turned gym locker room for the better half of the summer. Every other day, I would run in the file room, hold my breath, and magically file the amount of documents in one tenth of the time it had taken me up to this point. If this was a job performance strategy, it was working. Although by this time every one of my friends had endured the disgusting tale of Connie and the smelly bike shorts, I still had not worked up the courage to ask Guy Smith to move his clothes. To me, that was too mortifying of a task, even though *I* wasn't the one in the wrong, and *I* didn't lack the common decency to have my junk sweat airing out for all to breathe.

But one day, I decided enough was enough. To show Guy once and for all that it was not Ok to have the office assistant smell his bike crotch sweat, I decided to take matters into my own hands. One Thursday afternoon, I borrowed a bike from my best friend who lived nowhere near work and in my rattiest gym clothes, I biked the 10 miles in to work. It was July and before I even got out past the first mile, I already had sweat dripping down my face. By mile three I was exhausted and started to get heat stroke, but I pushed on, using my stubbornness as my only motivation. Mile ten, I glided into the parking lot and plopped the bike along the building. I climbed up to the second floor, dizzy and dry mouthed from the bike, not to mention I smelled like shit. Shuffling to the HR department, I walked right into Guy's office, took off my shirt Mia Hamm style, and tossed it in his face, gasping, "Here-dry this out, would ya?" and coolly walked away. Noticing I was tired, Tom scooped me up in his arms and carried me off to the lunch room where he bought me Gatorade as blue as his big charming eyes.

Ok. None of that happened at all. But that's the type of story I would daydream about as I was passing out from the odor in the filing room. In reality, I had spent about a month enduring the stink. That is, until the one fateful day when I walked into my sanctuary to discover a pair of half-assed hidden underwear drying off next to filing cabinet 'A-G.' One sight of an old man's drawers was all it took for me find my voice. I fled to Tom and told him the situation. He saddled his horse and rode in to deal with the smell and at high noon, he shot the guy on the bike. Or he just emailed him, I have no clue actually, but I did get my filing room back and Lysol'd the shit out of it until it felt clean. *Which it never did.*

After I found the courage to speak words in the office, I quickly realized it was a lot more fun talking to coworkers than it was sitting in a filing cabinet room by myself. The thirty-something ladies were the closest to me, both in seat distance and age, so I slowly worked my way up to talking with them.

Latisha was a thirty-year-old HR Specialist who had a love for cursing almost more than myself. She swore every other word when she was upset but always had a calm tone to her voice. Like a mother who was yelling at her kid in public- you knew you were in for a beat down, but first there had to be no witnesses. Plus she hated Gladys the orange eater more than I did. Latisha was the best.

Marcy was also in her thirties and we bonded over our Mexican-ness. She was sweeter on the surface, so you would naturally choose Latisha first if you were picking partners for something like Hunger Games, but that would be the wrong move. Marcy had a sweet demeanor, but she would absolutely destroy you in a fight. Between the two of these ladies, I would feel safe walking down the street in a bad neighborhood at night. That is why in my head I nicknamed them FEMA-because you would need the federal government to step in after these two wreaked havoc.

Outside of work we had zero things in common-FEMA were in different stages of life than I. They had kids and houses and IDs that weren't fake. But working with these ladies was the most fun ever. We would draw pictures of orange eater, make up names for people in the office, and eat lunch together. I learned some prime workplace bullshitting techniques from these ladies that you simply cannot learn in the classroom.

We also talked. A lot. They were like the older siblings of the workplace I desperately needed. It worked nicely, because I would listen, and they would tell me about their lives. I heard so much about their relationships, raising kids, what people do on the weekend when they aren't trying to find people to buy them liquor, it was all fascinating.

I loved talking with FEMA because it gave me the needed dose of daily social interaction I wasn't getting in school. As a commuter student, and a quiet person, I wasn't great at making friends. In fact, I only have two people that I met from college who are kind enough to not have de-friended me on Facebook, neither of which

I have spoken with since graduation. The trouble with making friends wasn't because I was some sort of freak- I'm so beautiful and fabulous and funny and virtually flawless in every way, so that's definitely not it. The problem with making friends for me was that A. I didn't live in the dorms so I couldn't be all like "Hey everyone! Foam party in my room!" or whatever you do in a dorm. B. Classes were on the quarter schedule, so in ten weeks, class was over. Ten weeks to make a friend? It took me from kindergarten to fifth grade to get in good with my best friend Alicia, so ten weeks was clearly impossible for making friendships. Plus, once you get older, it becomes more and more difficult making friends. Now that I'm nearing 80 (mid-thirties, but it feels older), I'm old and set in my ways and already have picked out my handful of friends. God help the next new acquaintance that suggests we get dinner- I'll look at them as if they're the MAC counter girls trying to convince me to do a 'free' makeover. Friends? No thanks. Already got some.

Summer was great and fun, but then I had to move away. As the busy season rolled around, I was assigned to actual work that required a computer, so I was moved next door to my own 'office' that was a small room visible through a shared window. This was nice in that I could see Tom leave his office and have plenty of time to look busy before he walked around and came into my room. But it was not nice because Gladys would often press her nose and paws against the window and peer down to try to see what I was doing. Then she would mime out whatever she was trying to say, which I would always pretend that I had no clue what she was saying until she gave up and resumed eating her lunch.

My new job duty required inputting driving logs on an outdated software system that still had a black screen with green lettering. There was the internet, but it was heavily blocked to avoid viruses. This was 2005. They might as well have asked me to use the Dewey Decimal system on my smartphone to look up when the next showing of Gone with the Wind would be at the local theater. Blah. One feature the electronic rock did have were the old Windows games- *Freecell, Hearts* and *Solitaire*, where you could personalize your game by choosing a card style. I preferred the beach theme cards personally, but would occasionally switch it up just for fun.

Wait. Does anyone even play Solitaire online anymore? I just downloaded it and Holy Christ, is that a time suck. It feels so wrong and dirty playing on your work computer as if you are flicking off your boss with each turn of the card. At least sitting on Facebook all day results in some form of social interaction- solitaire served no purpose other than seeing the cards jump up and down after you won. And remember when you could control how fast the cards jumped? What the hell was that? The more I think about it, the more I am grateful every day for the waste of time that is Facebook. God bless you Mr. Zuckerberg, God bless.

Anyway, about a month of me going pro at Windows Solitaire, there was a computer update that conveniently took the games out. So that left me with my logging software and Windows Works, which wasn't hooked up to a printer so unless I wanted to find a floppy disk, I wasn't getting any homework done.

It is often quoted that necessity is the mother of invention; well I needed the internet for distraction. I don't know what I did or how I did it, but I was somehow able to pull up the internet out of that old crappy computer. I remember the word Moxie and needing to use a new browser format and restarting it a bunch of times. But after one full Friday of messing with the thing, I was finally able to surf the Net, which I promptly used to email my friends long chain mail quizzes and old GIFs of flowers that sparkled. The rest of the day was spent on Myspace and Livejournal. It was magnificent. I do not have an accomplishment on my resume that I am anywhere near as proud of as I am for figuring out how to log on to the internet on that computer. Sad? Yes. But not as sad as the Emo Livejournal posts I used to write, which is why that account no longer exists.

Things were going splendidly in my new office with internet until the day I got a roommate. Sam was one of those out of shape quiet types who looked way older than he was. To me at the time, everyone older than 25 looked ancient, but a quick trip to the filing cabinets showed me that Sam's 49-year-old face was only 36. He was an accountant and did not like to speak, which I think is why they shoved him in the back with me.

I quickly hated Sam. He was totally cramping my style, not to mention affecting my Solitaire score since I could no longer play with a witness nearby. I tried to befriend him, saying weird things to him in the morning like, "hello" and "morning," but he didn't really respond, more so just grunted. If I was hired for a job and told I had to sit in a tiny room with a really pretty girl, I'd be pumped. But Sam wasn't about that life. He just wanted to work. And work stressed the crap out of him. He would often pound his fist on his metal desk whenever something was wrong. It was hard to understand how anyone could get stressed at a place as slow paced as LDVN, but that was the type of person he was. I imagine everything in life stressed him out, like if his pillow was too soft at home or if the sky was too blue that day. Life is hard sometimes, I get it, but you don't have to be a cry baby and pound your fist dude. Suck it up.

The most animated I ever saw him was when a person called his cell phone (A friend? Brother? Mother? Cat?) once and he started discussing Star Wars. This really happened, I'm not making some lame joke about nerds, or ripping off a Big Bang Theory joke, I swear. Star Wars Episode III: Revenge of the Sith had just came out, and they were discussing the plot line in depth. That was the most I ever heard him speak.

What Sam lacked for in conversation he made up in gas. Throughout the day he would drink a liter of Mountain Dew, and instead of burping aloud, he would burp in his mouth and let out a long, slow exhale of the burp, filling the room with the scent of warm, digesting Mountain Dew. Sexy. This constant act of extremely loud exhaling dubbed him the nickname, "the whale" which, if I ask my friend Cara (the one who also worked there for a brief time) "Hey, remember the whale?" we both cringe with disgust and burst into simultaneous laughter. I would run and tell FEMA stories of how I wanted to harpoon him and that Mountain Dew would spill into the room, drowning me so that they would see my dead body floating through the shared window as I gasped for breath. They agreed that burping was definitely as bad, if not worse, than loudly eating oranges, and we created scenarios in which we could lock Gladys and the whale in a room together so we could limit their annoyance to each other, freeing the world from burps and old lady chewing sounds.

When I wasn't listening to a whale breaching, I was in class. Sophomore year had just started, and being a marketing major, it meant that I was going to start taking business classes. DePaul University has two main campuses- the pretty one in Lincoln Park with the cherry blossom trees and a quad where students sit and read in the grass, and a downtown campus among the giant buildings and stores galore. All the business classes are downtown and this was my first year venturing down on my own. Say what you want about an away college experience, but after my first trip on the L to the loop campus, I was hooked.

Going to school downtown in Chicago made me feel awesome. I felt like a fancy business woman that you see in movies on a cell phone hailing a cab and saying things like "merger" and "latte." Can someone say hotshot? Even though my destination was to Accounting 101, I still felt super cool in a backdrop of skyscrapers, museums and Starbucks as far as the eye could see. It was a stark contrast to the Dunder Mifflin style setting of LDVN. That and the annoyingly long commute from downtown to work is what made me question whether it was worth the gas money, or if they had any cool jobs in the city that would give me money in exchange for work as well.

Another reason I was itching to leave was the lack of work. I'm pretty certain that if I played my cards right, I could still be employed full-time at LDVN living a nice, stress-free life doing office work. But at

19 I was ready to start a fancy career. I wanted something exciting, high paying, and cool to say at family parties. What no one told me was that even the fancy cool looking careers weren't necessarily fun, and that working with people you enjoyed talking to like FEMA was a gold mine in terms of long term happiness. But I wanted to drink espresso on the L and wear business suits with shoulder pads. So with a heavy heart, I gave Tom my two weeks, found him a replacement, and said goodbye to the first job that I didn't mind.

The whale was probably thrilled to have his burping room all to himself.

Office Translator

THERE ARE A COUPLE of words and phrases I have come across in the workplace that have a very different meaning than how they are perceived. Here is a list of some more commonly used ones, with a true definition of how they are used in the workplace. Note that the word synergize was not included because that is a made up word used by managers to make you hate yourself for not pursuing your life as a rock star.

Office supplies: Treasures from corporate that are meant to be stolen and used for personal use.

Reorg: Latin for, "Hold on to your ass." A reorg, or reorganization, is a restructuring of the departments and rankings in the office. Teams may be reduced, or combined, leading to months of speculating, searching public calendars for clues, and asking everyone in the office with a pulse if they know what's going on. Reorg's are never good and always end in a surprising twist that no one saw coming. Think of The Hunger Games, but with more terror and bloodshed.

Deck: This is a term for a PowerPoint document. There is no known reason why it is called a deck, but one can assume it was misspelled by one vowel somewhere along the way in an email and it stuck.

Business Casual: There is no clear definition for business casual, yet every HR handbook in the world has some loose definition with poor examples. In any dress code, the male outfit is used as a clear example (no polo shirts, khakis allowed, no cargo shorts, etc.), and women clothing examples include ridiculous examples such as "no midriffs." For the love of God, what woman in their right mind would wear a belly shirt to an office? No one, that's who. Some places have very strict definitions of business casual and force men to wear ties, while in other offices, business casual means you can wear jeans and a dirty t-shirt, just so long as it doesn't expose your belly button.

Summer Dress: See business casual. The only difference between the two is that men can wear polo shirts. There is no difference between the two for women unless you are a woman who loves men in polo shirts.

Emails: These are tiny pieces of your boss's soul that he or she has hidden and you must destroy by replying and banishing them from your Inbox. Yes, your boss is Voldemort.

Conference Calls: Synonymous with the phrase 'waste of time.' No matter how much your company pays for their phone system, the person calling in always sounds like they are lost at sea, breaking in and out over static, and you have to spend 10 minutes calling each other back so that you can continue hearing every other word that doesn't cut out. I was once on a conference call where my boss's bird squawked loudly in the background, only it was magnified and it sounded like she was being attacked by a flock of parakeets. That was the most productive call I've been on, because I spent the whole time learning how to control my laughter while other people were talking.

Meetings: Soul sucking time sucks of suckity suck. The only solace is if there is free food, which you have to pretend you are less interested in than the topic being discussed.

Performance Review: A time to utilize creative skills by reflecting on how little you've done in the past six months and rewriting it in a way that makes you seem god-like and essential to your manager.

Coffee: Life source at the office. Usually comes in disgusting forms, a conspiracy by Starbucks somehow to make you find them and buy the expensive stuff.

Candy Dish: A bowl with small items of sugar that people are more drawn to than any drug on the planet. I've seen people of all walks of life attack the candy bowl at work as if they had been stranded in the stairwell for days without food. Candy: making reckless savages of people since the beginning of time.

Personal Calendars: The most exciting thing to pick out, and the most dreadful thing to use.

Sick days: Time used to call off of work and nurse a hangover, watch the rest of your Netflix binge that you didn't finish Sunday night, or to sleep in because you did finish your Netflix binge on Sunday night.

Doughnuts: A sure fire way to get noticed and liked in the office, that doesn't involve s-e-x.

Cleaning people: The nicest people in the world that should be treated with the utmost respect and kindness. You can tell whether a coworker is an asshole if they don't acknowledge the cleaning person. You can also tell you are staying too late if you see the cleaning person emptying out your garbage can.

Company Culture: Whether you can yell and swear in the office.

Happy Hour: Ironically named, because if you are in need of a happy hour experience you certainly did not have a happy day.

It costs ten times more to acquire a new customer than it does to retain an existing one. I once used this to convince a coworker that he should buckle down and propose to his fiancé. Shortly after, he did. I'm pretty sure that it was all thanks to my sage advice.

The customer is always right: This is only true if you are the customer. If you work in customer service, you know that the customer is an utter moron, and you are amazed that he or she is able to pick up a phone to call you, because they are so DUMB.

Let's circle back on this: This means that the person, usually a boss, saying this wants to ignore the issue and hopefully it will go away. They want you to stop talking about it, yet they can't just say, "No bonehead, we are never going to do it." so they give an illusion that they will get back to it at another point in time, leaving you thinking the issue will be resolved, you naïve fool.

Have a good weekend: Translation: "I've had to look at your face for five days in a row and I finally get a break. Don't come back on Monday because I hate you!"

Did you have a nice weekend?: Translation: "Dammit you came back. Now I have to sit with you in a meeting."

Stale Doughnuts and Career Paths

LIKE I MENTIONED BEFORE, college wasn't my time to shine. Basically, my strategy was to get in and out as quickly as possible. The only time that plan was foiled was one late spring day when I entered the revolving doors at DePaul's downtown campus and got my flip-flop stuck in the door, capturing me and some dude in the doors. It took about 1 minute in real time but eleventy-hundred minutes in anxiety time for me to pry my shoe out of the door, releasing us both from our glass cage. I don't remember much else from college other than the hot teachers and my English elective-creative writing 101. That class was awesome in so many ways especially since my other classes that quarter included Accounting 102 and some type of Business Ethics (Sidenote: Business Ethics. Psshhh. What a load of horse caca).

Because of this, I spent the first half of my college years not making any friends, since I was too much of a quiet nerd during class to talk to my peers. Instead, I would either drive 70 miles west to Northern Illinois University where my boyfriend and his frat friends would constantly have something exciting to do, such as in-door beach parties and flippy cup tournaments. I realize now the irony of leaving Chicago to find fun things to do in DeKalb, Illinois, but when you don't have an ID and aren't a devout Christian who knows how to have a jolly time sans booze, you go where the kegs are tapped, and in this case it was in the middle of a corn field.

Towards the end of my sophomore year, terror struck and my boyfriend dumped me, taking with him my resources of weekend fun. But through times of despair rise determination, and with that, I got myself a fake ID, pierced my tongue, and proceeded to find the best bars in the city that were kind enough to let a heartbroken, booze crazed nineteen-year-old into their establishments to forget about her troubles.

Turns out, all of those bars where shit dives. And I was their Miller High Life Queen.

When I wasn't drowning my heart in cheap beer, I worked downtown at an accounting firm. Pearson, Gibbons and Associates, run by two women- one pretty and heartless, and the other who dressed like a comedienne in the 90s (Read: vests.) and also heartless. It was the most professional looking office I had worked in, much better than the pits of the Luigi's phone room, and there were zero biking shorts on any of the filing cabinets. Success! I hid in a cubicle near the entrance, answering phones and pretending to file, a skill I had much experience in.

When I wasn't pretending to work, I was super busy creepily staring at one of the accountants, Josh. Josh was the Jim Halpert of the office- awkward smile, goofy hair, and the only decent looking one around. Had he been walking down the street or in a crowded bar, I wouldn't look at him twice. But just like the stale, half-eaten donut that's left in the box at the end of the day, coworkers become more appealing when there are no other options around.

I did my best to flirt- asked him random useless questions, sought his advice on where to buy lunch on my break, you know, the normal desperate stuff people say when they are trying to get noticed by a coworker. Actually, I kind of used Jim Halpert skills in attempts to get him to notice me. If he had a candy dish of old jelly beans at his desk we'd be married by now.

But none of my 'flirting' worked and things moved nowhere for 3 months. Then one day the company held an event at U.S. Cellular Field (now called Guaranteed Rate Field), where that other, non-Cubs baseball team plays. Being a northsider, I hated the Sox. Not because I pay attention to baseball in any way, but more of a hyper-regional preference. But even though the event was on the Southside, I was dying to go because it was in a fancy skybox where everyone would be dressed up and in my head, I would be drinking cocktails in comfy leather seats next to Josh who would instantly fall in love with me. In reality, I went to the event, got stuck handing out name tags and passing out desserts, and was treated like the help by my heartless bosses. I was not allowed to drink and had to go home by the 6th inning because the heartless owner thought it best to have only clients and accountants there for the rest of the party. It's hard to flirt when you're handing out mousse, but it's damn near impossible to flirt when you are considered as part of the wait staff instead of the firm. I lost hope and ran off to a bar where baseball jerseys were considered proper dress code.

I had almost given up in getting to spend quality time with Josh until fate gave me a second chance and one of the accountants had a going away party. *This* was going to be it. I would get to dress hot, had a real ID at this point and would get to bring a girlfriend for added support. I envisioned a romantic scene where in between a round of jager bombs and kamikaze shots, Josh would glance over and realize the one he'd been looking for all along was sitting fifteen feet away from him, wearing a telephone headset and cheap polyester pinstripe pants.

I arrived at the bar, looking hot as hell, boobs galore, and was the coolest I have ever been. I was taking shots, telling stories, flipping my hair, it was perfect. Josh clearly had noticed because my friend said he was in love with me so of course I believed her. The group decided to head out to another bar. Walking out of the bar heading toward the cab, Josh promptly slapped me on the ass, then as soon as we arrived at the next bar, proceeded to puke out 3 jager bombs, 2 kamikazes and 4 Miller Lites all over the table.

The Office did not prepare me for this.

After that I couldn't look at Josh in the face. Actually, I could, but didn't want to for fear of gagging at the thought of seeing puke all over the four top. I could never be with a guy that couldn't handle his liquor. Luckily, I was moving on to a marketing internship at another company, so the fact that he wouldn't be in viewing distance meant his hotness plummeted back down to a 3. And that was the closest I had ever come across to an office romance. Somehow, I think Jim and Pam's love story is a load of bull. Nobody finds love in an office, or anywhere else where there is fluorescent lighting for that matter.

A few months later, my boyfriend and I were together again and life was back to normal. I started at the marketing internship which is left off of my resume simply because I cannot recall what I did there even enough to make something up. I think it had to do with mailing CDs of a video game? And making coffee? Obviously it was not a groundbreaking moment in my career. Although, I started drinking coffee there, which is pretty momentous, so there's that.

What was groundbreaking at the end of my junior year happened, shocker, in a bar.

Up until this point, my goal in college was to be a cool advertising executive. I wanted to be a creative type that came up with cool jingles like Ray Liotta in *Corrina Corrina* when he came up with the JELLO ad, or Mel Gibson when he was the cool Ad Executive in What Women Want, before he became a crazy person in real life. Did I have any graphic design skills? No! Did I have knowledge about the industry whatsoever? No! Did I want to sit around dreaming up the next great beer commercial? Yes! Somehow, I felt that I had enough credentials needed to launch my career. I planned this all out, often confiding in my friends, until one night we were at Kelly's pub near DePaul in Lincoln Park and one of my girlfriends was talking to an older guy (read: by older I mean he had a job that paid him enough to order bottled beer that wasn't on special). This guy clearly wanted to get in her pants and definitely used his job in hopes of at least getting her bra off. But as soon as he said "I work at Leo Burnett," my friend (who heard me talk about advertising enough to know that Leo Burnett was one of the top ad agencies in Chicago) yanked him over to me and made him tell me everything he knew about how to land a job in advertising. Cock blocked but flattered at least one girl at the bar was looking at him, Dan obliged and gave me the inside scoop into the world of advertising. Turns out, he didn't so much work for Leo Burnett as he did for their sister company, but it was as close as I could get to an actual agency contact. He told me the setup of what creatives (the one thinking up the ads) do, explaining it's more likely I would start out as a junior account manager, and proceeded to explain how I'd be better off in account management anyway, since most of the creatives he knew were coke heads. Pity. If only I had shown initiative back in my phone room days and snorted the white stuff up my nose, I'd probably have been making jingles by now. Why didn't anyone tell me the way to a career is through the nostrils! I felt like Mel Gibson should have prepared me better for this.

I kept up with Dan for a while, but since I hadn't taken Business Communication 101 yet I had no clue how to properly network outside of a bar, and let that connection fizzle away. After talking with him at the bar, I was starting to think maybe advertising wasn't for me. I wasn't completely naïve to believe all agencies were coked out crazy houses, and I realized that Dan was more likely a former college kid like myself with dreams of making jingles, now stuck in a sister company looking over excel sheets of ad revenue budgets, but the more I learned about agency life, the more it felt like I wouldn't mesh well.

That didn't stop me from making a complete ass of myself to the industry.

The scene was Wrigleyville. I was out with my girlfriends for a friend's 21st birthday and doing what is normal in Wrigleyville- acting like a douche and getting wasted. We started the night out at *Casey Morans* and quickly walked in and out of *Trace*, before we stopped in at the *Cubby Bear*. The *Cubby Bear*, is essentially the culmination of the shit show that is Wrigleyville. Underage drinking, frat dudes being asshats, and stickiness. Lots of stickiness all over. I was drunk enough to start in on my usual post-pre-game, pre-puking rant about what am I going to do with my life after college. I was confiding in my girlfriend, contemplating how I wanted to make six figures by the age of 25 (Sidenote: me in the past? You're an idiot). By mid-rant, I had to pee. I had been holding off on breaking the seal because at the *Cubby Bear* they have bathroom attendants. I haaattteeee going to the bathroom with attendants. I hate the idea of having someone hear you using the washroom, and being right there when you get out, like, oh hey, no you didn't just fart, that was totally the other person. Here, have some gum. Then I get drunk and feel bad for them that they have to spend their weekend handing out paper towels to stupid drunk chicks and I try to overcompensate by smiling at them awkwardly. It's a mess.

But in this particular bathroom on this particular night, I was distracted from my personal nightmare by an ad placed inside the bathroom stall. It was for a new flavor of vodka, which, back in 2007 was a relatively new concept, unlike today where vodka comes in every single flavor you can imagine, including wine flavored vodka, which even as a former college drunk, sounds like a bit much.

I was crouching over the toilet without making contact with the seat when I read the bottom of the ad. For some reason, it had the name and phone number of the agency that created the vodka ad, and they were based in Chicago. In my completely un-sober frame of mind, I thought, clearly this agency is listing their information because they want smart, perceptive women to call them up and inquire about their company. It's 1AM? Even better! That shows initiative and the fact that I can dial a phone right now shows maturity. OF COURSE IT DOES SOBER BRAIN, OF COURSE IT DOES. So I dialed and got an answering machine to the agency. I was surprised I didn't get a person on the other end, assuming there must be some excited coke head sitting around making up a new jingle, but apparently they all went home for the night, or were out to buy more coke. Unfazed, I left a quick, to the point message stating my reason for calling, ending with a cold closing on how I wished to learn more about any opportunities they may have available. It went something like this.

Hello?? This is Connie! I called about your ad in the Cubby Bear ssstall, I like the strawberry vodka and think you did a versy neice job with the ad. But you need more peoples to make ads! You should totally get an intern and I can do that! I can get an internship with you. Ok I have to wash my hands now, you call me ok? I love marketing! Byyyeeee! Go vodka!

Rookie mistake. I forgot to leave a number. But I didn't notice and walked out of that stall so confident that I wasn't even intimidated by the bathroom attendant looking at me funny.

By the start of my 4th year in college, I had taken several marketing classes, but was still unsure of what to do once college ended. I had rushed through college to get it over with, but with advertising looking less and less appealing I needed a career path. Aside from the countless shady sports marketing jobs posted on Craigslist, most of which met in a parking lot outside downtown, I had no idea what else one could do with a marketing degree. I was getting a minor in sales, but if I wasn't willing to talk in an advertising group, there was no way in hell I'd be able to sell crap to people. That involved smiling! No dice.

I was two steps away from a midlife crisis at 21 when I found a job at DePaul in the Enrollment Marketing Research department. I'd be a student worker with a flexible schedule, and as far as I could tell from the interview it involved no sign holding on street corners and paid $1 more above my asking price. MO MONEY MO PROBLEMS!

Working in the EMR group was the best gig I had had to date. It didn't offer discounts on cheap clubbing outfits, and I couldn't score free pizza for flirting with a cook, but there were other perks. For example, I actually got to do stuff that involved marketing. On a team of 6 I was at the disposal of any researcher, and got to help with projects like designing surveys, or making PowerPoint presentations. To anyone over the age of 21 this undoubtedly sounds boring, but to a young person who prior to being a student worker did zero actual work that was of importance, these were exciting new grown up things, and I was learning a lot.

For example, did you know it's best *not* to use a neon background on every single one (or any, for that matter) of your PowerPoint slides? Or how you don't have to have every single bullet point zoom in from a corner of the screen? Seems strange, I know. But that's what I was learning, among other skills, such as what exactly market research entailed.

Before senior year, my main perception of market research was through taste testing at focus groups my mom would sign me and my sister up for as a kid. Although she will probably be sainted for being the nicest lady ever, she always told us to lie, lie, lie and say we liked everything to the screener so we'd get chosen for a focus group, earning the sweet reward of up to $30 for an hour of tasting things like new Kool-Aid flavors.

Turns out, market research was more than taste testing. It was a way to critique and analyze all those ads that coke heads spent months of blow working on. And it was a way to find out what a company was doing right or wrong and how to fix it through research studies. Basically, market research was a way of supporting your claim. Take for example this common phrase.

Your sister's a whore.

The punch at the end using the term whore is the advertiser's work, with their fancy lingo and use of sentence structure. Now as a researcher, here's what I do.

Your sister's a whore because she banged the majority* of the dudes on the block.

*Source: 2013 survey of every dude on the block, valid percent n=19 since the guy at the end of the block was on vacation with his parents in Florida at the time of the survey.

Fun, right?

What was not fun was where I was located. Being a student researcher as opposed to an office assistant had perks. I didn't have to clean anything or fetch things for people for one. Well, sometimes I had to fetch things, but it usually involved a please. Progress! Despite all that, I still got stuck in a crummy 'work station.' Every other employee sat in a cubicle or office around the perimeter of the floor, but in the center was a large work space and food/coffee area. In the space, loud fax machines would go off and people shuffled in and out to make copies. In the other space next door, there was a fridge and coffee machine. I was in that room. So countless times throughout the day, an employee would walk through, putting me in the awkward dilemma of looking up and acknowledging their presence with painful small talk, or continue working. I chose painful small talk because I have the attention span of a two-year-old and turn toward anything that moves. It was the perfect set up for being constantly awkward and completely unproductive.

Talking about the weather and lunch options paled in comparison to the smell, however. Directly in front of my computer was the refrigerator where everyone kept their food. This fridge was from the 80s and had not yet been cleaned since it was purchased. So every time someone opened the fridge, a waft of old food smell consumed the room, leaving me gagging and disgusted.

Having learned absolutely nothing from smelling bicycle shorts for months, I did nothing to fix the smell. After about 2 months of this I finally worked up the nerve to bring it up to the office manager, who promptly took care of it by having the fridge cleaned out. Problem solved. That's when I learned my first takeaway from working as an adult- always speak up, especially if something smells like garbage (which I should have learned from the bike shorts incident, but alas, I was young and shy.)

But in all honesty, I would have gladly dealt with the fridge stank longer than that for one simple fact. I had the best boss ever. Joy was the senior market analyst in the department and had all the traits of a Disney Princess. She had nice hair, she never got angry or annoyed, and she was so sweet I was half expecting woodland creatures to follow her in each morning as she broke out into song. She bought me cookies from Starbucks for doing the smallest task and always gave feedback in the form of extremely kind compliments. Working for her made me excited to come in to work, and I was the least late in to the office each day that I have ever been.

One time I was working on a project that required few brain cells. It was a mapping project of all the survey respondents based on their address. You would have thought I was the first cartographer ever the way Joy and her colleagues thanked me for my work. It made me want to work harder and bend over backwards to do a good job. Plus, like I said... cookies.

As my final year was ending, I was taking my last set of marketing classes that I was planning to ever take again. That spring quarter, I took Tools for Marketing

Analytics by Professor Zafar. He started out the class by saying that we can remember how to pronounce his name like suffer because that was what he was planning on making us do. Then he described the tools for data analysis as 'sexy.' He was by far my favorite teacher. Prior to taking the class I was struggling to understand what the hell it was that analysts do. It was like in *Friends* when Chandler would always say his job title, and no one knew what the hell it meant. By the end of the class, not only did I totally get what data analysis and statistical reconfiguration meant, I wanted to do it and be Chandler Bing when I grew up. Minus the third nipple.

After 52 classes, 2 fake IDs, and eleventy billion Miller Lites in red solo cups later, I graduated from college. In the fairy tale ending, there would have been an opening working for Joy in the EMR department and I never would have had to face an unpleasant job again. In reality, I would go on to face scary bosses, horrible work hours, crazy deadlines and enough crap to give me a twitchy eye and a 401K.

At least I knew what to do when the fridge starts to stink.

Market Research and Evil Villains

WHEN YOU GO TO HELL, you don't realize you're there until it's too late. It's not like Satan walks in and says, "Hi!!! I'm the devil. Welcome to hell, you sit over there by the people who listened to their iPod too loudly on the train when they were alive." Instead, you wander in as the temperature rises slowly, degree by degree. It isn't until you're burning up that you start to panic and realize you're in the worst place in creation with no visible escape route in sight.

That's what it was like working at Brownward Mill.

I had done the impossible. Within a month after graduating from DePaul with a B.S. (heehee, 'BS') in Marketing, I was sitting in an interviewing room at a well-known market research agency. I was sporting my new black Ann Taylor Loft suit and a Calvin Klein work bag that I had purchased at a discount from Marshall's with some graduation money. My resume was hot stuff and barely needed padding thanks to all the jobs I worked during college. The position I was being interviewed for was as an assistant research executive, working on the household cleaners account to do things like analyze brand awareness, ad recall, and purchasing patterns, or in other words, figuring out how to get people to buy toilet bowl cleaner from a little cartoon bubble.

The whole structure of the company was confusing as hell, and it seemed like I had 15 bosses. But the salary and benefits made me feel confident I could figure it out (5 figures! Whaaaaat???). So as confused as I was when they were showing the organization chart that listed all the VPs and dozens of other confusing titles, I quietly contemplated how soon I should go to the Toyota dealership to pick out a new (used) car that could get me all the way from home in Chicago proper to the western suburb of Naperville each day.

I was so happy when I got the offer that everything turned into a lucky item. My suit was lucky, my bag was lucky, the Kleenex I used to wipe the nervous back sweat off of me in the car before I went into the interview was lucky. I was so happy not to be a post-college wanderer, and that after countless amounts of crappy jobs, I, Connie O'Reyes, was finally in a real adult job that would be the start of my fabulous career as a businesswoman. There I was, 22, and already had my life figured out.

Apparently there was a group of other young twenty-somethings who also had just figured out their lives at the same time as I. We had all been given the title of ARE (my first of many corporate abbreviations, this one meaning I was an assistant research executive, or possibly the assistant to the research executive. I so get you, Dwight K. Schrute. I. get. you.) The first day was orientation, where seven other ARE's and myself were starting with the company we would be committing our lives to. The HR orientation leader spent the morning going over the corporate history, corporate mission, corporate culture, corporate strategy, and finally, compensation and benefits- corporately of course.

The office building was enormous and consisted of six floors. After our initiation where they branded the company logo on our asses, we took a tour of the main floors. At the main level, there was a Kelly green painted reception space with a large reception desk and modern looking office plants all around. These weren't your average office ferns, but some imported looking shit from Asia. Super fancy.

Below in the basement was the break room with refrigerators, toaster ovens, a sink, and several microwaves. In other words, a kitchen. Why seeing a kitchen in an office building seemed so cool, I have no clue. Perhaps it was that I still could recall the stench of the DePaul fridge and knowing that I would be far away from my coworkers' moldy yogurt put me at ease. It was thrilling.

Next to the kitchen was a large, spacious room with a pool table, pinball machine, and air hockey table. Forget the microwave; this office has a game room! I was surprised that even though it was lunch time, no one was playing. That was a red flag. Pro tip: if you are ever interviewing for a job, ask to see the office. If they have a fun break room with games, get the hell out of there. I am not kidding. Run. What I didn't realize then was that the more fun and exciting a company tries to make its office look, the worse off their workers are.

It's like this Hawaiian bar near the city called *Hala Takiki*. Inside it is a festive Hawaiian themed restaurant with straw huts, native Hawaiian music, and fish tanks all around. The wait staff dresses in tropical Hawaiian shirts and leis. But look closely, and you can see that the staff are by far the most miserable looking people I have ever come across in my life. That pool table was my Hawaiian shirt, and instead of getting lei'd, I was about to get screwed.

On the second day I got to meet my 'team,' as well as learn that a business buzzword for a department is a 'team,' which is stupid. I envisioned a group of Bears football players suited up, sitting in a pod of cubicles, waiting to hand off a PowerPoint down the hallway into an end zone. Instead, it was a team of three other women, all with varying degrees of insanity and evilness.

At the top of my team was Joanne, our team's VP. Joanne was a mixture of Lord Voldemort from *Harry Potter*, Miranda Priestly played by the lovely Meryl Streep in *The Devil Wears Prada*, every middle school mean girl that has ever existed and that scary eye thing in *Lord of the Rings*. Joanne had been working with the household cleaners team since I was born and somehow bewitched them into thinking that she was not pure evil. For some reason they loved her, so whatever she said was gold, leaving her in a very comfortable position with Brownward Mill and her job security.

Next up was Roooosita. This woman was cray cray. Like, for real. She was the only one on the team I had met during the interview process. She spoke like Sofia Vergara and looked like Sofia Vergara's butt ugly kid sister. Rosita was blunt, making it clear during the interview that she wasn't going to babysit me while I learned the ropes, and that I'd have to catch on quickly if I wanted to move up. She also made it clear that she was an opportunist, and as soon as the chance presented itself, she was ready to jump as soon as a higher position with more prestige presented itself. This was my work mentor.

Kim was a mom. She had two young kids who were old enough to wipe their asses but not old enough to make their own dinner, somewhere in that age range. Kim was bright as hell, but she worked from home most of the time on special projects that had nothing to do with me, so I didn't get a magical *Lean In* mentor relationship with Kim as I had hoped. But one time she brought in brownies that she baked using only brownie mix and a can of black beans, and they were the most delicious brownies I had ever tasted. So, there's that.

I saved the best for last, which was Maggie. Maggie had been with Brownward Mill for one year and was also an ARE. Upon meeting her, Maggie also looked like the busiest and most flustered one on the team. As Rosita took me around, she explained to me who Maggie was and that she would be the one I would work with the most, since she would be teaching me everything I needed to know. I was nervous and excited to meet her, but when we walked up to her desk, she gave me a half turn and said, "hey" before turning around to type out the rest of an email. Normally, I would have taken that as a sign of great offense, but Maggie was my age, had the same brown colored hair as I did, and by the looks of her pale skin, she was Irish just like me. We were so going to be work BFFs but she just didn't know it yet! Luckily I was able to win her over approximately one month later when we were preparing for a meeting and she asked who was bringing the report in, to which I replied, "IDK, my BFF Jill?" This was a line from an old Cingular commercial, and was a hilarious commercial at that. Maggie replied with a loud, "What did you say?" In a tone that asked, "Did you say something funny and out of context in this meeting room that I can laugh about? Because if you did, we are going to be great friends."

After that, we instantly became work friends and soon realized we both shared a deep dark secret, which was that we both were obsessed with the MTV series, *The Hills*. In case you are weird and had a life during 2006-2010 when the show aired, the premise is that it was a 'reality' show following Lauren Conrad and her tanned friends from her original show, *Laguna Beach*. The young women were all starting out their careers in various industries in Hollywood, while struggling with boys and other difficult things, like finding a place to drink smoothies. It was by far the best 'reality' show on earth, ending tragically in the final scene where they cut to a Hollywood set, leaving viewers wondering if it was reality TV, or just a show all along. One of life's great mysteries to this day.

The Hills was the one thing that would change our otherwise intelligent vernacular down to the high pitched screams of a bunch of twelve-year-old girls. It was the perfect non-work thing that let us sit in our cubes and discuss, giving our over-worked brain cells a break, just long enough to contemplate whether Heidi should get back with Spencer. Talking about *The Hills* was similar to how people, not me mind you, but people do yoga- to relax, recharge, and to get ready for the shit that's about to go down throughout the week.

Aside from having my first work friend established, I also experienced having my very own cubicle. One that I didn't have to share with another intern, or a whale, or any other species. It was my very own real estate in a sea of computer desks.

My cubicle was the first in a row of desks heading towards the windows. I had Maggie across from me and all the managers behind me, leaving too much exposure to waste time on the internet. My desk was a curved L shape with a desktop computer and two monitors. The second week, I brought in picture frames, colorful desk organizers, snacks for emergencies, and all sorts of crap to make this desk unique from the hundreds of other similar desks in the office. Looking back, it was more like I was decorating my burial plot with flowers, but we'll get to that later.

The first few months went by ok. Maggie and I worked closely, especially the first few weeks when she was hand-holding me through every complex job duty. It was immediately clear why Maggie looked busy; she was doing the work of six people, including Rosita's job, which was always piling up on account of Rosita scouring the internal job postings hourly. Maggie was in charge of five brands and their tracking studies, which meant each week there would be survey results of internet panels of crazy people who sit online filling out surveys for some minuscule reward like movie tickets. Maggie would have to make changes to the surveys, upload new ad images to match that week's advertising that was airing on TV, deal with the ad agency that was making the ads and the client who was paying for the ads, and everyone in between. Then she would have to deal with the survey people who put the survey into the internet, and another department who pulled the results out of the internet. And when that was all settled (which it never was, because when you are dealing with 90 different departments, odds are something's going to get messed up somewhere), she would have to make disgustingly long PowerPoints explaining what all the data meant in great detail, broken out in different ways. And now I was there to do all this as well, in addition to our other full-time job, which was to attend meetings.

It wasn't the workload that killed me at Brownward Mill; it was the crazy ass amount of meetings. Ok, maybe it was the workload, but the meetings were extra punches to the throat. On an average day, I would have three meetings, lasting at least a half hour each. Multiply that by five working days and you get 7.5 hours, which is an entire work day. That means, to do our average amount of work, which was always over the standard 40 hours, we would have at least one day's worth of meetings. This sucked the life right out of me. One time, I shit you not, I had a pre-meeting to discuss what would be discussed in the meeting, the actual meeting that went on for 2 hours, then a post-meeting recap to talk about what was said in the meeting. Then, Rosita, who somehow missed all the meetings, needed to be caught up to speed on things, so we had an impromptu meeting at her desk to discuss the meetings. So one entire day of my life was spent just meeting about a meeting so much that my Outlook calendar reminder was constantly on my desktop. How freaking sad is that. I could have been on a boat that day. Or gone rock climbing.

By Thanksgiving, Rosita found a new position, and Kim was rarely in the office, what with kids to feed turkey to and cornucopias to make out of twigs. That left Maggie and I exposed to the treachery of Joanne. Until this point, Maggie was able to shield me from the evil death rays that would shoot out of Joanne's eyes, but with our team down to a size of 3.5 people, and with eight parent brands and over twenty product brands (What the hell is that you ask? Think of Windex, then all the different types of Windex products you have under your sink- wipes, sprays, car cleaning sprays, sprays to wash your eyes out when you make the mistake of watching any show on Bravo, etc.). So our forces were down and I had to fend for myself.

Whenever the client needed a weekly, monthly, quarterly, or yearly report, I had to talk to Joanne. The bigger the PowerPoint presentation (or 'deck' as we called it. As in, this deck is 120 pages long, FML), the more room for error that Joanne could find. Knowing what I know now about the world of market research (which is, it's not freaking rocket science), I don't think I screwed up as often as it seemed. However, every time I walked away from Joanne or read her email feedback, I felt incompetent and angry, which is a bad combination.

Luckily, my home life was chill enough to balance out work. I was still living at home (free rent! Whut whuuut!) and that guy I was dating was working in a nearby suburb, so occasionally we would leave early to commute together and eat breakfast. Actually, I think that only happened once, but still, it was nice. Driving in the snow 35 miles to work however was a bitch and a half. One night, it took four hours, I kid you not, to get home. That was the day where eating at a Denny's was the highlight of my day; another sign that things were not as good as the paycheck made it seem.

For Christmas, instead of having time to do things like Christmas present shopping and drinking hot cocoa by the fire, my team was preparing for the end of the year wrap up. This meant extra work, all of which fell on Maggie and me. I survived by putting up Christmas decorations, including a cubicle wall-sized Christmas tree in the shape of our Brand Dynamics pyramid, with Awareness at the base and Bonding at the top. This sad little Christmas tree was the only bright thing in my office, and I was starting to see that. But I kept getting promises that they would be hiring new people, we'd be a team again, and things would get better. It was like a Hallmark Christmas special, but instead of hoping dad would come home from the sea in time for Christmas, I was hoping for another coworker to take some shit off my to-do list. God bless us, everyone.

What happened next wasn't surprising, but it still crushed my soul. Tragedy struck two months later, and Maggie decided that working on a team that was nonexistent and putting in 70+ hour work weeks was not as great as getting the chance to work with a normal team. So she moved to a different account, and I sat alone with a handful of decks and the desire to drink Multi-Purpose cleaner until I was as dead as the 99% bacteria it claimed to kill. Worst Valentine's day ever.

Luckily, it wasn't a complete tragedy. Maggie moved only one cube wall away, so I could bother her endlessly, although she was often busy making new friends on her team and leaving at 5 o'clock to go home and have a life. But with Maggie leaving, the company realized they probably needed someone other than a girl who had been working a grand total of six months to carry on a million dollar account, so they brought in two people- Kristen and Stacey. In the course of my time there, no men worked on the household cleaners account. Did they think that this was women's work? Did Joanne hate men and they were afraid she would eat their heads like a praying mantis? Who knows.

The arrival of Stacey was like the arrival of a cowboy riding into town, based on the 20 collective minutes I've ever watched a cowboy movie. After a big scare that they would bring back Rosita to the team, word got out that Stacey would be coming in, working two days a week, the rest working from her home in Iowa. Yes, Iowa. As in a state that is not Illinois where we were located. According to the rumors, Stacey was once a senior research associate who transferred off her last account to go work as a bounty hunter in Iowa, but missed the life of a market researcher, so came back to Brownward Mill to work on my team. I'm making 90% of that up, but that's the mystique that was Stacey.

When Kristen came in on her first day, I was typing out an email, gave her a half turn, and said "hey" just as my predecessor did to me eight months prior. If Stacey was the quiet, mysterious cowboy, Kristen was the wild, gun slinging gal that came in with a loud laugh and a love for beer.

This was perfect timing because with all the shit Joanne was giving me, I was at the point of not giving a shit. That transitioned into beer lunches. When we could escape between meetings, we would always go to *Houlihan's*, because one beer there was about 32 ounces, so we didn't feel as bad for drinking what was technically one beer. And it didn't matter when we would stay for a long lunch and have two beers, because either way, we would be working late, so who cared if we took an extra 20 minutes for lunch?

You would think that by adding two people, who could put in approximately 140 hours per week collectively, that my hours would have improved. Not so. Somehow, and I have no clue how, but somehow things got more difficult. It was as if as soon as Joanne saw happiness on the team, she found new ways to take the work we were doing and double it.

The night before Joanne had to present the quarterly findings for the Furniture care products, she decided that we had to add the new wipes campaign, even though two weeks prior when we asked her, she said no. That led to my first all-nighter, where Stacey and I stayed at the office until 1:30 in the morning. Every hour after 5pm, I kept thinking to myself that this was a joke. Someone was going to walk in any minute and say just kidding Connie! You can go home now. But it never happened. Stacey, who had been working on the account for one month, stuck it out with me but staying at work any time after 7pm is awful, no matter how much support you have. I had to call my mom around 10, to let her know I wouldn't be home in the foreseeable future. It sounded like a conversation between a young Civil War soldier and his mother, desperate for the war to be over.

Me: Hello Maw? It's me, Constance.

Maw: Constance? Oh, Constance! Heavens to Betsy Constance where on earth are you?

Me: I'm at the office Maw, and I'll be here all night.

Maw: Oh my dear, Constance. Why oh why must you stay?

Me: It's this damn deck Maw, it just won't end. They say tomorrow it will be out, but who knows, who knows.

Maw: Oh Constance, do be careful, I worry about you so, ever since you were a baby I knew I'd be sitting here, worried about you and that terrible Furniture care deck. How long does it have to be?

Me: It looks like we'll be seeing 120 slides by morning.

Maw: No! Constance no!!

Me: Now Maw, don't you fret. I'll be home in time to see the tulips blossom along the riverbanks, and you me and Jimmy John can pick apples on old man Henry's apple orchard. You'll like that, wontcha, Maw?

Maw: Oh Constance, yes. Do be careful. And try to order something for dinner.

Me: I just had some leftover California Pizza Kitchen I found in the fridge Maw, I'll be alright.

We got the deck out. It turns out Joanne didn't have enough time to talk through wipes after all, so she had a chance to send us in-depth revisions the next day to get it finalized. If this was a war, that was the cannon that gave me a fatal wound.

I would have left a lot sooner if it wasn't for all the fun I was having working with Kristen. At 5'10", black hair and perpetually tanned, Kristen was a tower of fun. She would do things like make hats for the little toys that sat on my desktop and think of insane ways to decorate people's desks for their birthdays. In the world of cubicles- decorating a person's desk for their birthday is about as fun as it gets. It usually involved poorly photoshopping the person's head on the body of something, like when it was Maggie's, we put her face in the cast of *The Hills*, obviously. Or we would fill the cubicle with balloons, wrap everything in sight, you know, the type of antics that are amusing when all the fun has been removed from your life. I wonder if inmates decorate their cellmates bunk with toilet paper streamers in prison?

Kristen also liked to drink as much as I did. On beer Thursdays, she would run out to Jewel and pick up a six-pack or two and plop it on my desk. This was perfectly acceptable since Miller Lite was an account for another team, and because the company had that pinball machine in the basement, it was the 'cool' company that didn't mind if you drank, just as long as you do it in the office and don't EVER, EVER leave. Fridays we would have 'Scramble Friday,' because that was the day Joanne would come into the office to shit on us, and we would always have to scramble around. It was a way of making a terrible day manageable, and Kristen was the best shipmate to throw a crazy party on a sinking ship.

In July I was expecting a promotion. I had been working on a horrible team for a year and saw four coworkers come and go while I stuck it out in the trenches. Kristen thought I would get it, Maggie thought I would get it, we were all set to get our celebratory beer lunch drink on just as soon as I had my one-year review.

I was brought into one of the meeting rooms with Stacey, who had been my boss of exactly four months, and our division's VP, who handles one year reviews, at least ones where the person in evaluation hasn't had a steady team to work with and the person who does work with her is the devil. I walked in thinking this would be a breeze, smiling dumbfounded as I plopped down in my chair. That's when they handed me a PIP-personal improvement plan. I had only come to know this term when Maggie would tell me crazy stories of past Brownward Mill employees that no longer worked there because they received a PIP, which was a notice saying hey you suck, we're about fire your ass.

I was shocked.

I was silenced.

I was devastated.

I WAS PISSED.

They stated the reasons for my getting proverbially kicked in the balls were because my work wasn't to the point to where it should be after a year. Comparable to the rest of the AREs, they were absolutely correct. My work wasn't as good as a junior level researcher who had a full team, a boss who was there longer than they were, and who was doing a normal workload of a person in their position. I wasn't thriving; I was merely surviving. And now I was being given an explanation of why that wasn't good enough, why my year spent of working late and lugging home laptops to work on weekends was not good enough.

My reaction afterward was so melodramatic, I could have been brought in on *The Hills* as Connie, the overworked crazy person from Chicago, in to break the hearts of millions of LA guys. I left the meeting silent, and instant messaged Maggie who shuffled me out of the building so fast, she should work as a bomb rescuer. She took me for a walk around the outdoor space of the building- a lovely area with a man-made pond and picnic benches for people who had time to sit for lunch. They were empty.

Before this day, I had never cried at work that anyone knew of. Although I rarely had time to piss, I would use the bathroom stalls to cry after a harsh email bashing from Joanne occasionally. But never in public. PIP day was different. Maggie and I circled the building, where I proceeded to sob uncontrollably (if I were on *The Hills*, this would have made for an excellent close up of my mascara running down my face.) while cursing out everything. Maggie made me walk another lap.

It seems that in a time of tragedy, people do weird things that they don't even know how or why they did them. After I calmed down to the point of not hyperventilating, I just wanted to drive. Unfortunately, that day I had zero gas because I was rushing to get to the office for my first meeting of the day, which was now over. I drove over to the nearest gas station to fill up, and that is where I called Joy. Not devil Joanne, but Joy, my former boss from DePaul. I don't even know how I possibly had her phone number in my 2008, non-internet accessible phone, but for some reason, it was there. We hadn't talked since my last day, and my pleasantry emails to her had quickly dwindled as I was spending most of my time apparently not working hard enough, so to call her out of the blue was odd. The conversation went something like this:

Me: Hello Joy? It's Connie. The old student worker person.

Joy: Connie! Hello! Oh, it's so nice to hear from you! How are you doing?

And then I proceeded to sob uncontrollably into my Blackberry.

Joy was kind enough not to hang up on me. Instead, she calmed me down and explained how everyone in her department came from a bad work situation, and that I would get through it. I told her I wanted to quit, and she softly suggested I think things through, promising to email me resources from the university that could help me look for a new job.

I walked back into the office. Kristen was hoping I'd come back with a gun to shoot Joanne. I was numb with hate. The rest of the day was me staring blankly at a computer until Kristen, Stacey and Maggie pulled me out of my chair to take me out for drinks. This is the absolute best thing you can ever do for a coworker who just had their ass handed to them on a piece of paper. We went to a nearby patio bar where I downed Miller Lites by the gallon-full. I was formulating my plan to quit- no notice, no niceness, nothing. Stacey, my boss mind you, supported my decision, and promised a letter of recommendation. It turns out she was getting pushed out as well, as Joanne didn't care for any strong women who were competent.

So with my sidekick Kristen at my side, after we drank all the Miller Lite in the western suburbs, I went back to work to collect my things. Like two drunken ninjas, we snuck quietly in, walking past the dark rows of empty cubes. I pulled up my Outlook as Kristen packed my things and proceeded to write the most eloquent email to HR ever written. I cited days where I worked well beyond what was required of me, gave a timeline of the people the team had lost, and detailed multiple examples of over-work, summarizing that Joanne was to blame for it all, and without significant changes at the top of the team, the company would continue to bleed out money spent on turnover.

Then I hit send, CC'ing everyone in my PIP meeting and as many VPs as I could find in my Outlook address book.

And so ended my career at Brownward Mill. When I first started, I thought my last day would be me gray-haired, getting a watch and a toast among all my young AREs I would mentor over the years. Instead, I spent it drunk with my things in a box, laughing with Kristen in the parking lot as the street lights shined down on us.

Bathroom Break

Warning: If you're above poop jokes, this chapter is not for you. Move on to the next chapter where the content isn't as messy (heehee).

One of the things at work that makes my brain think 'OH MY GAAAAHHHHDDDD NOOOOOOO!' is taking a crap when other coworkers are in the bathroom. To me, making my bowels activate in the presence of people who I'm supposed to try to get to respect me and value my opinions is the complete opposite of what I am trying to achieve. I've been training myself not to give a crap (get it?), but that has not worked out so well.

The problem is that your sight, sound, and smelling senses are all alerted at the same time, so there is no escape. Obviously, women like to think their shit don't stink, as referenced in the wonderful rap song 'Roses' by OutKast, but it does. And yes, you can always use an air freshener, but the automatic ones don't target the point of contact, and picking up a Febreze bottle after washing your hands is like waving a flag to the world saying, "Yeah that's right, I did it. That's my poop you smell." So really, there's no solution that I have encountered to eliminate the smell.

The other problem is the sight of it all. Now if you've got yourself a low flow toilet, may God have mercy on your soul. Those things leave trail marks that are impossible to ignore. I've never clogged a toilet at work, thank goodness, but if I did, I would have no clue what to do. Call someone? Tell the receptionist? I'd rather quit and be poor. There aren't even plungers around to help out the heavy hitters; you just have to run and flee.

Luckily there are ways to get around sound if you are so lucky to work in an environment that cares about your humility at all. When I first started working at my latest job, I went into the bathroom after setting up my belongings in my new office, only to discover a bathroom setup as near to perfection as can be- there was a radio in the bathroom. A RADIO IN THE BATHROOM. Clearly, CLEARLY I was in the presence of geniuses at work. Listening to Rihanna's latest hit single on KISS FM has made it infinitely better to go to the bathroom because I can escape through the music and pretend I am the only one around for miles.

One of the greatest bathroom experiences of my life happened one day when I was working at a job that shall rename nameless for fear of them finding out that I ever used the bathroom. There was this woman; we'll call her Claire because I am not that mean and I don't want karma to creep up and make me shit my pants one day in retaliation. Claire was a very fancy, professional looking lady. She had one of those fancy long bobs that cascaded down towards the front. She always had on a nice Calvin Klein dress or something equivalent and always looked crisp. She appeared very smart and good at her job which had to do with external communications to different PR agencies. As I came to work with her, I realized Claire wasn't so much smart as she was good at taking other people's work (mine) and turning it into her own, which I guess is a type of smart. Still, I marked her on my list of enemies and thought of ways to expose her for the fraud that she was when I wasn't busy doing other things like buying Christmas presents on Amazon during work hours.

I was in the bathroom, practicing my art of invisibility when Claire walked in at the same time. This is important to the plot because it reveals that I saw and identified who was in the bathroom at the time of the crime. We each went into our stalls, and just as I found the courage to release my bladder despite the audience, I heard what was arguably the loudest, most unflattering fart sound I have ever heard in my entire life, followed by, "Oh my."

Now granted, 'oh my' is about the classiest freaking thing someone could say when they've just made the most thunderous butt noise in the world. But that didn't make up for the fact that I just heard fancy pants Claire, in the next stall, SHARTING out her lunch. (For those of you with an upper class vernacular, sharting is the act of farting and shitting at the same time. Now back to your tea time.) I was stunned, and couldn't move because I would either A) laugh uncontrollably or B) poop myself from the shock.

Claire ended up relocating out of state for a different job soon after. I'm 99% sure it was because she was embarrassed by the bathroom incident. I would have quit for sure if I sharted that loudly with a coworker in the next stall.

As gross as it was, Claire's colon movement was a great eye-opener to me, and it was a truly humbling moment in my life. It made me realize that no matter how smart, how beautiful, or how utterly confident a person can be, everyone's poop can be loud and smelly. Kind of like that 'everyone's grave is the same size, you can't take it with you' concept, but with more grossness.

I've decided there needs to be an endpoint to my fear. So when I'm near retirement (or hopefully, when I get so famous from this book that I never have to step foot in an office bathroom again), I'm going to become one of those wild women who actually talks in the stall and gets all rowdy, even though the people around her would prefer to sit in silence, willing her to go away. When that day comes, I've created a list of funny things to say to make the trips more entertaining. Feel free to paste these on your workplace's bathroom stalls and encourage others to get over their fears to talk freely on the pot.

Things to say to coworkers when you are in the bathroom at work:

- "I hate you Potbelly's!"
- (When someone starts to go) "Oooo- someone's been drinking their eight glasses of water!"
- (Out of complete silence) "They'll never find me in here." And then giggle mischievously.

- (When someone enters the bathroom) "Run! Save yourself!" (Then from the stall, grunt in constipation.)
- (Out of complete silence) "My weight loss plan is pooping."
- "Ugh. Why does the flash on my phone never work?"
- "Jesus take the wheel!" (Then kick the door for dramatic effect.)
- (If someone else makes a noise) "WHOO! Somebody had tacos for lunch!"

Watch Out for the Antelopes

SINCE PUNCHING PEOPLE in the throat at work (or I guess anywhere else for that matter) is generally frowned upon, I often fantasize about what it would be like to seek justice on those that have wronged me. Actually, 'wronged me' sounds a little too strong, like I'm about to go all Dexter on people and murderize them. Okay, I never actually watched an episode of Dexter, because I was busy during its run watching *Breaking Bad*, PRAYING that Jesse would not die after each episode. Aaron Paul, if you are reading this, you are the greatest actor alive, and you were even cute when you were beat the hell up, which was like *always.* Let's be best friends!

That went a little off course. But, I'm leaving that in since it's a pretty good segue into how my mind wanders. Had I gone on, I would have imagined Aaron Paul inviting my friends and me on his yacht, probably named Jane, or Crystal Blue, and we would be partying it up 90s rap video style. That's just how things work in my mind.

When I'm commuting to and from work on the CTA, my daydreams are based on whatever I am listening to at the time. When Fall Out Boy was big, I was called out on stage when the drummer was unexpectedly unable to perform, and I would magically do a kick-ass drum solo to Dance, Dance. Whenever I listen to Britney Spears, I am at a crowded party (super skinny and fit of course), and dance in a crowd, with all eyes on me. Most of the time though I am in some hip-hop routine battle that randomly breaks out in the middle of a crowd at a party, and people are all like, "Oh shit! That white girl puts the ass in fantastic!" Or, you know, whatever cool hip-hop people say. But then it's my stop, and I have to put these dreams aside for 8 hours until it's time to go home.

At work, whenever a colleague acts like a jerk, there's not much one can do in retaliation without getting reprimanded themselves. Even though sometimes it might make sense to punch your coworker in the throat for being a total ass to you, as a classy human who doesn't want a police record, that might not be the best way to go. This is why instead of acting on my anger I often sit around thinking about how the story should end, justly and in my favor. I'm not some creepo who talks to themselves and has pictures of these people hidden in my desk drawer with a big red DENIED stamp over their face, I just think of how things should end after a shitty situation, which is usually in a dance-off.

Here are some of the best scenarios of the worst situations I've been in, with even worse humans who deserved to be punched in the throat, but more creatively.

I don't know how to start this story off other than, SO THIS BITCH....

So this bitch Cass was the heartless lady I mentioned earlier (Remember? 90s comedienne in a vest?). It was 2005, the same job where I was fawning over that puking guy, Josh. Cass was the forty-something-year-old VP of the tiny accounting firm, where I was the administrative assistant. Two things stick out, (aside from her blonde bowl haircut and vests with shoulder pads), which were that she made me wear a dog cone and threw change at me.

Fine. It wasn't an actual dog cone. But I felt like I might as well have been wearing one considering how ridiculous the phone headset was. At max, the firm received two phone calls a day when I worked there, while everyone else was using this thing called 'the email.' But Cass insisted that someone man the desks at all time, so when the office manager was out running errands for Vests McGee, I had to take the phone headset and sit there with it on my head. That's another thing, she wouldn't even spring for two headsets, the office manager and I had to share a device that was shoved in each other's oily ears multiple times throughout the day. This was the closest thing I've had to unprotected sex, and it left me worried that I'd get some ear transmitted disease. An ETD if you will.

The other thing actually did happen. This asshole had the audacity to throw change at me. Me, a human.

One day Cass called me into her office and sounded very flustered. Thinking this was some form of accounting related emergency that could only be fixed by the aid of a part-time administrative assistant; I made the executive decision to dash in, without passing off the headset to the office manager. When I arrived, Cass told me she needed a Dr. Pepper.

She did not ask me to get her a Dr. Pepper mind you. Nor did she passively mention how thirsty and tired she was, giving off a hint that if only she could get the quenching taste of a carbonated beverage with 23 flavors, mixed with caffeine, so that she might finish her file which would produce a large amount of revenue for the firm, thus securing my much-desired paycheck. Instead, she told me she needed one, leaving me to stand there awkwardly with a headset on my head without my phone in sight to process what I was to do.

Also, there was something wrong with her neck because when I approached her, she didn't turn to acknowledge my presence the way people with necks do, which is to turn it in a way such that the head is facing the other person in the room. Instead, she rummaged through her briefcase and *tossed* change on her desk in my direction.

Oh, hell, no.

You may find by now that I am somewhat of a hyperbolist, and that is true. But I can honestly say that I am at a loss for answers when it comes to the question of naming a person that was more rude to me than Cass. Joanne was a beast, yes, but she at least looked me in the eye when she was giving me a verbal beat down. Those 15 seconds in Cass's office were more degrading than the time I had to sit next to dirty bike shorts. She may as well have had me dance for her in a monkey costume, that's how low I felt as I picked up her change, my face contorting into that clenched way when you smell something foul in the air- your tongue pressed to the roof of your mouth, lower lip pushed up while your eyebrows furrow deeply to the point that they might touch. That is the face I get when I think of Cass and her Dr. Pepper.

I've long fantasized what I would do to seek my revenge on Cass someday. The best I could come up with is being a super successful person who finds themselves dripping with cash and is in need of an entourage to handle all my money. I would go to her office (because she would still be working there years later, most likely in the same vest) and would walk in wearing a million dollar outfit. Possibly a gown one might wear to the Oscars. Hell, maybe I'm on my way to the Oscars, WHO KNOWS? Anyway, I would be dressed awesome, a complete juxtaposition to the vest, and walk into her office with 50 cents. I would just have signed a contract with the president of Pearson, Gibbons and Associates as my full-time accountants, and I would walk into Cass's office with my crumpled up tax documents, *toss* them on her desk and say, "I need my taxes done. Oh, and *fetch* me a Coke." AND THEN WALK OUT. BOOM. IN YOUR FACE!

Why would I give her business after holding a grudge with her all these years? I honestly don't know. Perhaps I need to rethink this one a bit.

Tamale Burps

Junior year in high school is a super important year if you want to have a future. At the start of the first semester, the teachers all scare their students by warning, "You better do well in this class because this

will be the set of grades colleges are going to look at."
Then you realize you're in trouble because your English
teacher just ended a sentence with a preposition.

It was finals week, but I was eager to get a jump
start on summer job hunting since every teenager would
soon be finding themselves in need of a three-month
employer. I really wanted an office job so I could sit
around in an air-conditioned room if possible. Because
job websites weren't popular yet, or perhaps I just
hadn't known they existed, I looked in the want ads for
employment. Two days before finals, I worked up the
nerve to call an ad that was asking for office help. The
man on the other end of the line explained he had an
office that handled a variety of things- insurance, real
estate, and a bunch of other businesses that sounded
legit. He told me to come in after class the next day so I
could try it out to see if it was a good fit. Happy to not
have to fill out a job application, I agreed.

Looking back, this was so incredibly foolish.
Although the office was on Addison, a major street, I
did not know the office, or who if this old man was a
creep. For all I know he could have been in the
'kidnapping girls who didn't want to take their Algebra
2 finals' business, and I was walking into his well
thought out trap. I don't even think I told my parents
what I was doing after work. How stupid is that! The
more I think about it, the more I realize I should have
definitely been murdered. So what happened next was
really not so bad.

The office was next to a Laundromat, as are all
places of employment with promise. It was halfway
from school to work, a perk that I thought would be
useful. I walked inside to a dead plant cemetery, and

walls lined with wood paneling. Both the plants and paneling were first placed their circa 1970, as was the old man sitting next to a pile of papers and files.

This guy had to have been 93 years old, at the least. That was good for me because although I had no upper arm strength whatsoever, I was fairly certain I could easily defend myself should this man attack me, simply by flicking his legs with my index finger. I will call him Mr. Adam since I cannot recall what his real name was and I am fairly certain he was the first male on earth. Mr. Adam explained to me that he handled several businesses, and each time he explained this he would add on another one. By the end of the day, he was in the insurance-real-estate-commercial-lending-actuary-patent business. I'm pretty sure whatever the business once was, they closed up quite a while ago and forgot to tell him. He was still using carbon paper and typewriters to make copies. I felt like I was traveling back in time. Which, let's face it, suppose one day one of us stumbles across the magical way to time-travel, be it with an old Doc and his weird car, or a strange vortex found in a closet. Despite what TVs and movies portray, the odds of stumbling into any significant moment in history are rare. Most likely you'd end up watching some random guy getting his teeth cleaned on a Tuesday instead of seeing the Roman Empire or dinosaurs.

It also would have been a lot cooler to time travel if I didn't have finals the next day. I was contemplating my choice in timing as I was doing super important assistant tasks like walking to a file cabinet and handing Mr. Adam a piece of paper, or organizing his papers on his desk in order of the least amount of food stains on it. About two hours in, Mr. Adam had an important task and asked me to go across the street to the sketchy tamale stand to get him a tamale, and a plastic spoon.

I considered fleeing as soon as I got outside, but I felt too bad for the old man. Plus, I've been drunk enough times to know that sometimes all you need at the end of the day is some greasy Mexican food to make things better, so I obliged and brought back his dinner. This led me to my next task, which was sitting and watching the ninety-three-year-old man eat a tamale with a spoon. As weird as it sounds, that moment in life gave me clarity. It made me realize that if I ever wanted to amount to anything, and not rely on jobs in the want ads that resulted in watching a guy eat a tamale with a plastic spoon, that I'd have to get my ass in check and focus on school and work.

And then the old man started burping.

Sketchy tamales are gross. Sketchy tamale burps are even grosser. He wasn't even coy about it either. Each time he let out his stomach sounds, he emulated Barney Gumble, famed burper and Homer's friend on *The Simpsons*. With each gassy breath passed, I hated myself more and more for not being at home studying for Algebra 2. I hated that I had made a stupid decision and that I didn't have the balls to get out of it without feeling super anxious and awkward. I stuck it out the last hour, and headed home, reeking of pork and cornmeal, exhausted from the anxiety I had given myself.

I called Mr. Adam's office late that night when I knew he wouldn't be there to tell him I wouldn't be returning. It was an ass move since I had told him I would be in the next day, but I at least had the good sense not to return. I don't even have a revenge story for this one, because it's not nice to be mean to the elderly. But someday when I get into a position of power, I'm going to make my young impressionable assistant go to that sketchy tamale place, and we'll both eat gross tamales, and burp in my enemies faces, together, thus changing the course of history once and for all.

Pick your Enemies

Taking the train downtown as a young lady sucks a big one. At 21, I usually needed a buddy to go to the bathroom with at a party for companionship. Do you know how many times I've sat on a bathtub ledge talking to a friend while they pee? Hundreds. Because God forbid I stand alone at a party for two minutes, that would be awful. So taking the CTA downtown each day for class was no picnic.

Summertime on the train is particularly dreadful. I'm not even going to get into the foul stench of people who haven't developed the concept of bathing and deodorant, or the PFN syndrome (pale flabby knees- it's an epidemic that happens in Chicago every first day of spring where women pull out their short skirts, revealing the damage that winter has done to their eating habits and the effects of a lack of vitamin D. I need to credit my friend Cara here for co-inventing this term, further proving that being alone, even in a thought, is less awkward and a million times more fun with friends.)

The part about summer on the train is the difficulty of dressing oneself so as not to attract attention from creepers. And let me be clear, I ain't no hoochie mama-

I dress just fine and have never been reprimanded for going against dress code. I am a rules follower to the T, so dressing office appropriately is not a problem. The problem is that a large portion of CTA patrons are perverts who enjoy leering at women who are dressed basically in anything other than a garbage bag. I wouldn't put it past some if they found garbage bags to be sexy as well.

This particular day, I was in a button down, blue dress shirt, and gauchos. What's that? You've blocked out the disaster that was loose-fitting capris from the mid-2000s? Yes, they were the longer version of culottes, but they were comfortable and fabulous, and a million times more comfy than skinny jeans. God, I miss gauchos.

I was sitting on the train, minding my own business, when I get the feeling something is happening outside of my imaginary bubble and the notes I'm reading for class. I look up to find a man in his late 30s, short, dark hair, ugly face, just staring at me and grinning. Grinning, by the way, is the number one sign that you are definitely dealing with a grade A creepster. It is the main identifier to determine if a potential pervert is looking at you pervertedly, or just looking in your direction because there is minimum safe eye space on public transportation. Grinning? He might as well have pulled it out right there for all to see.

If you've never been leered at (which, if you are a woman, yes you have) let me tell you, it is a disgusting feeling. Several things rush through your head in a matter of seconds. Why is this guy staring? How long has he been looking at me? Is he going to try something scary? Did he follow me here? What if he gets off at my stop? Why is he not turning away? Doesn't he have a mother who taught him better? WHY THE HELL IS HE STILL STARING AT ME????

The other, disturbing aspect of getting eye groped, is the knowledge that you have not been selected for any special reason. This guy wasn't looking at me because I was pretty- I was wearing oversized pants and a collared shirt for Christ sake. I wasn't proud of my appearance in any way. My clothing choices in college were a hot mess, having recently been released from 12 years in a plaid uniform, I had no clue how to dress properly (still don't). Knowing this, I often wore what was comfortable and easy to throw on when I was running late for class, as per most college students tend to do. This gross dude decided that looks didn't matter, and the fact that I had lady parts was enough for this asshole to think it was cool to stare down a girl going to class, and that I was put there as an object for him to look at, like a free, live version of a girly magazine, except I wasn't getting paid to pose, and I was wearing gaucho pants.

So what did I do to detract my creeper and seek justice? Nothing. Like I said, I was afraid of my own shadow, let alone standing up to a stranger in public. I gave him an angry look, which to him probably just looked like I was giving him a sultry stare, but he didn't budge. This guy had the balls to just stare me in the eyes and grin until my stop came and I leaped off the train as fast as my flip flops would let me move.

Ever since that day, I've been waiting patiently for my next creeper on the train, because I know EXACTLY what I am going to do, and have it all mentally planned out. The next time I am face to face with a nasty, disgusting creep who is staring (and grinning), I am going to do the least sexy thing I can think of:

I'm going to pick my nose.

I have it all planned out. The dude will be sitting across from me, just like the original creep. I'll look up from reviewing a final manuscript of my latest written masterpiece, only to notice the guy staring me down. I'll start out by giving him an eyebrow lift as if to say, "What me? Why sir, would you care for a piece of this?" To which he will most likely lick his lips, another key trademark in creeperdom.

I'll lean in, staring him right in his soulless eyes, and sexily lift my well-manicured hand, pointing my index finger up. Then, I will go to town and pick my nose like I've never picked it before. Depending on the situation, I'll do one of two things; 1) If I have a clear exit and the guy looks slow/doesn't look like he would run after me, I'll flick my findings in his direction. 2) I'll wipe the boogers on myself because that sounds super gross and I think even those British guards who aren't allowed to move no matter what would even barf at that site. Either way, I would go full force, hoping that my actions will not only gross him out but make him reevaluate his life and consider that women he stares at on the train are humans that may not like to be looked at as if they are going to be molested any second.

Most likely though, the guy would get turned on, because that's the type of unpleasant miscreants you can expect to sit next to you on the train.

The Couch Surfer

Have you ever hated someone's face? Like upon first meeting them, you know. You. Just. Know. It's not a superficial thing; it's more of an internal animalistic instinct. That's probably why the first lion went up to an antelope and ate it. He knew that the antelope looked like trouble, prancing around, with its dumb, vacant expression. Have you looked at a picture of an antelope? They're so stupid looking. The lion could have been all like, "Hey, we'll just be pescatarians; it's cool, fish don't have feelings." But then one day an antelope came around, and the lion was all, "Oh hell no! Not this bitch. I'm gonna eat him." I have mother nature to thank for warning me about Janet by giving her a stupid antelope face.

Janet and I were colleagues, and from day one I smelled trouble. She was an annoying, negative, pain in my ass. We worked together for the state housing department, and if you're thinking, "Wait, what? We haven't gotten to the state department job yet!" Then I say gold star to you because that's not until the next chapter, but my hatred bubbled over early into this one.

Janet was in her late forties but looked like she was in her early sixties, so I had a nice warning sign sitting next to me each day reminding me to lay off the weeknight partying. She was on my shit list because not only was she annoying, but she was super unhelpful and unfriendly as a coworker, and would only acknowledge you if you could help her with her work. She was one of those types of people where you asked to borrow a stapler she would come back with an explanation of how it's not her job to keep track of office supplies and she's so busy that even if she did have one, she wouldn't be able to hand it to you and waaaaahhhhh. But if *she* needed a stapler, it was expected that the whole world unite to help her find one.

We sat next to each other in a cubicle setting that shared a low divider, so I got to see every irritating thing she did. She had a nose issue (cocaine in the 80s will do that to you) which caused her to be extra nasally sounding. She also had a Minnesota accent, but with the extreme nasal and the constant complaining, she was like the worst example of Minnesota nice. Minnesota probably kicked her out for not being nice enough. Yes, I'm pretty sure now that is what happened. She also dressed too young for her age, but I feel like you already put that together in your head, so I'll leave it at that.

What made Janet look ungodly old was her lifestyle, which she liked to brag about a lot. She was a couch surfer which she thought was super cool. If you don't know what couch surfing is, let me explain. It's when crazy people think it's safe to go on the internet to a website and look up houses people post who have a couch or room to spare. Unlike Airbnb, you often stay with a stranger, instead of renting out their house. Being alive to tell this story, I can say I have never used it, but I'm pretty sure these people have space in their homes for guests is because they chopped up their family who was living there and ate them for breakfast one day. Then they got hungry and were searching for more people to eat.

Janet preferred staying with men because of course that's safe. Every weekend that she would go 'surfing,' I'd wish a crazy story would happen to her. Nothing harmful of course, I'm not the crazy one here. Weird enough so she learned her lesson NOT TO SLEEP AT STRANGERS' HOUSES so that she wouldn't come back to work to brag about it.

Every Monday after one of her adventures, I'd ride the elevator up to work, envisioning what may have happened on her latest couch. Maybe the couch had bedbugs, and she had to stay home to wash her frizzy hair. Perhaps the couch owner where she stayed kidnapped her and made her watch old episodes of Barney the Dinosaur on repeat, never letting her leave. She would call the office in a frantic panic, and for some reason, I'd be the one to answer the phone. She would say, "Help me, Connie, I've been trapped by a crazy couch surfer, and I need your help!" And I would simply reply, "I'm sorry Janet, I'd totally help you but I'm busy looking for a stapler. Bye." And she would be trapped forever on a couch, and I would never have to see her again!

But then I'd get to my row of cubes and see her there, sniffling into her Kleenex and posting pictures of her in weird hats to her Facebook profile. That's the problem with my daydreams- they never actually happen, and instead, I'm left staring at the back of a coworker's head all day, counting down the minutes until lunch.

Why the State of Illinois is Going Bankrupt

A week after I quit Brownward Mill, my life turned into a sad country song. I had no job, my family dog got fleas, and someone stole the spare tire from my Rav-4. Pretend I had a pick-up truck, and you've got yourself a Country Music Award for best new artist right there.

I spent a month wallowing and watching rerun marathons of The OC during the day while functioning humans were at work. My parents were always nice and supportive and fed me dinner each night, but I'm guessing they were wondering at this time if they were ever going to see a return on that college tuition bill they just paid off as they watched me get up at noon to eat ice cream for breakfast.

After a few days of sulking and de-fleaing the house, I started searching for a new gig. Desperate to prove I was not a loser, I searched everywhere. Word to the wise of any budding marketing major fresh out of college- those Craigslist ads for Sports Marketing jobs paying $75,000 to start? That's not the Bulls or Bears, or hell even the Sox. It's a guy in a parking lot somewhere on the south side trying to sell illegal cable. Avoid it and go straight to your college career board- those are at least monitored enough to make sure you don't interview for a sketchy job like I did.

The job posting sounded legit- entry marketing position in downtown Chicago. It was located in the nice area of River North, and was located in a large brick office building, not down some dark scary alley. All exterior signs seemed to point to not being a scam, but here's how I figured otherwise:

1. There were a lot of applicants in the waiting room filling out applications. Jobs that are worth anything usually weed out the losers before they call them in to fill out an application. Since I had already sent my resume in, they should have determined whether I was a crazy person enough not to have ten other women sitting in a cramped office.

2. Everyone was a woman. Either this place was only seeking women for their big brains, or the employers were seeking out certain criteria. C cups at the bare minimum perhaps?

3. I didn't know what the job was for. The job description I found online was a vague marketing description that looked like they took the definition of 'marketing' and pasted it to the job board. Seems too legit to quit!

Once I completed the application, I was taken into a room with a guy in a room that had a desk, two chairs, and a glass cage with an iguana in it. I shit you not. Couple of things that should have tipped me off- the guy looked like a weasel, he had no phone in his office, it was very dim, too dim to do any paperwork, which coincidentally, there was no sign of him doing work from his desk anywhere- not even a scrap piece of paper with notes on what to feed the iguana. Nothing. I should have walked in there, looked at the iguana and walked right on out.

Instead, I sat there in my blue button-down shirt and year old discounted Ann Taylor Loft suit trying to figure out what the job entailed, to which the interviewer was very vague about. I don't think he ever clearly explained what the job consisted of, even though I asked a lot of questions to try and figure it out. I left them with my application, which I can't remember, but I'm pretty sure had my social security number printed on it, because I'm as smart as an iguana.

Nonetheless, I was pretty shocked they never called me back. Being young and self-conscious, I figured one of the other, prettier applicants, got a callback. Now, I check my credit score now and then fully expecting a large debt of foreign lizards to show up.

After my sketchy interview, I decided to be more cautious before sending out my personal information in the hopes of a job. The Illinois Housing Department (IHD) sounded real, so I sent in my application and waited. About three weeks later, I heard back, and after an initial phone interview, I waited some more before I got the in-person interview. Between sending the application and starting at IHD, it took about eight weeks. This was life giving me heads up, warning me that my time for the next year would go by like the interview process, slow and painful. But what did I care- I just wanted a salary to prove to my parents that I wasn't a bum, and that I was smart, despite what the douche canoes at Brownward Mill thought.

I was eventually hired to be a marketing analyst in a marketing department of four. Jack, the wise oracle of IHD, was there when Illinois built the first public housing development in the days of yore. Jack was in charge of the marketing department, which consisted of three women, including myself.

Aside from Jack was my direct boss and Jack's work wife, Laura. If Jack and Laura were married in real life, she would have poisoned his morning oatmeal a long time ago. I've never in my life met a person who was so quiet and pleasant speaking in public, but who ruthlessly hated her coworkers with a fiery passion the way Laura did. Finally, I had a work mentor to look up to. She used the word dick with Jack's name interchangeably, as if it was his nickname. Jack was a little pervy anyway, so if he ever did hear her, he probably wouldn't have minded her using that word.

Janet was also lying around, and she was supposed to help me get situated when I first started, but by 10 AM on my first day I realized she was useless and instead I would hang out in Laura's office, listening to her defile all the people she hated. We would talk for about two hours, and then it would be time for lunch, which quickly turned into a two-hour lunch once I realized Laura didn't give a flying shit (her words), and I would walk down Michigan Avenue, wasting away my time and paycheck care-free.

IHD was located right next to the river on Michigan Avenue, sharing a sidewalk with the Tribune Tower. But to get to all the good Michigan Avenue shops you had to walk down a bit to the Water Tower, which isn't a problem unless its summer and ALL OF THE TOURISTS are out walking at a glacial pace. I quickly learned that to get anywhere you have to walk along the curb, in between the street and the tulip gardens that fill up perfectly good walking space. Even though I never had anything to do, I always panicked when I would check the time and see I had spent well over the allotted one hour lunch, praying that I hadn't gotten an email from Jack calling me into his office. It happened like once, and even when he did it was just to pass the time explaining a project for hours that took all of five minutes. That was a typical day at IHD.

Even though it was clear that this was no corporate rodeo, I still respected the office walls and went to great lengths to give off the appearance that I was earning my pay. To accomplish this, I would do courteous things like leave half the files I needed to file away on my desk, showing that whatever I was doing (Facebook) was so important that I did not have time at the moment to finish my filing. All I can say is, thank God for computers. Seriously, WHAT did people do before personal computers in the office? How did they waste away eight hours Monday thru Friday without something to stare at and pretend to be frustrated with? The number of times I glared inquisitively at my Facebook feed to make a boss walking by think that I was deep in thought is literally in the thousands. I can't imagine life before computers; it sounds so hard.

Actually, if I lived in any period before today's modern capabilities, I wouldn't have made it. I often think about how quickly I would have been killed or burned at a stake for being so lazy if I was living in the olden times, especially before plumbing. Walk outside to take a dump? No thanks. While the isolation of pooping alone sounds nice, I'd probably be too lazy and want to hang myself, but I wouldn't know how to tie a knot, which is something I would have Googled if the capability were available.

I read the entire Twilight trilogy at IHD during work. Not on my lunch break mind you, but during work. When people in my life would ask how my day went, I would update them on where I left off. "Edward agreed to sleep with Bella! But only if he marries her! How could she not want to marry him?!?! I love vampires!!!"

Despite the low-walled cubicles revealing my shoulders and up to everyone in a 20-foot radius, I sat and read books about hot vampires that was meant for tweens. Three of them. I would sit there, looking down, keeping a file nearby to cover my reading so when a coworker came by to talk. Or if Jack would walk over to glare at me in his weird attempt to intimidate me but really made everyone look at him awkwardly, I would shove my book under a file and proceed to look as if I was reading a market summary. I thought I was pretty clever when in actuality, a more seasoned time waster probably would assume I was doing something more inappropriate, like looking at porn.

Even though I was reading trashy teen novels, I still had enough respect for the great state of Illinois to at least pretend I was working. My coworkers, on the other hand, did not. Janet was off surfing the net each day for her next couch to surf on, and my coworkers in the next cube row over would constantly shout at each other about what they would eat for lunch, followed by, "You're stupid!" So it would go something like this:

"Ian, what do you want for lunch?"

"Steak and lobster!"

"Ian you're stupid!"

Every. Day.

And then Janet would turn around and vent to me as if to say, "Can you believe these guys? They're so loud, I can't get my work done." And I'd be like, WHAT WORK? WE DON'T DO ANYTHING HERE. And then she'd go back to fixing her dating site profile picture enough to make it look like she was 30 instead of 50 (apparently hats and scarves are old people's secret cover-ups. Also, hats and scarves do not work. Like, at all.)

What I was hired to do did require brain cells, but very few. My main responsibility, along with brain dead Janet and angry Laura, was to review all of the housing credit applications and their market potential. You see girls and boys, when a housing developer wants to make a building, he or she can get credits (cash money) from the state if they promise to keep some of the units for low income tenants. Then, marketing analysts (that's me!) review their plan, along with the proposed area and neighborhood to see if it would be a good fit and good use of the state's money. Then, all the good applications go to board review, and in 9 months (or up to several years) a baby housing unit is born! My part in this took about 30 hours, twice a year. The rest of the time I did smaller side projects, and the most important job, avoiding getting trapped in Jack's office.

Jack, who was nearing retirement and had been for the past 10 years, liked to take innocent victims into his office for something obscure, like asking a nonsense question about an application. Then, he would proceed to trap you there for his own entertainment to hear himself speak, and would proceed to rattle on for hours and hours until your bladder would burst, or your eyes would fall out from boredom, and you would die. This happened rare enough that I didn't have to die every week, but it happened enough for me to develop the same boiling hatred Laura felt for Jack and everyone else in the office who didn't seem to enjoy getting lectured for days on end about the most useless shit you could imagine. To summarize, Jack was the type of person who would pull out a map and take fifteen minutes to look stuff up in it, instead of going on Google maps. Jack was the worst.

You would think that having a job that required few hours of actual work per week plus limitless hours of bullshitting would be every person's dream. But only three months in, I was already dying of boredom. In December it was too cold and snowy out to go walking around outside, so my hours indoors staring at Janet's head multiplied. And I hated it.

My idle hands wandered into a Blogger account, which had a viewership of about three: My best friend Alicia (of course), my other best friend Cara, and other best friend Emily. Variations of this website were made, each more eye blinding than the last. This was before the days of pre-made web layouts. You know what, it probably wasn't; I just thought using lime green as a background made me stand out.

When I rode the smelly Red Line train to work each day, I would occasionally pick up the *Redeye*. The *Redeye* is the Chicago Tribune's newspaper that was growing in readership in the mid-2000s and appealed to a younger 20-something demographic (and it was free-ninety-nine.) I remember the first time I was handed one by a newspaper vendor in college. Having mastered the streets of downtown, I was accustomed to avoiding peddlers of all sorts, so when a newspaper vendor waved a thin paper in my face, I shooed it off, until he insisted it was free. By the time I was working downtown, it had become a daily habit and was the perfect light read of entertainment, celebrity gossip, and local events that I never attended, but enjoyed knowing they were there.

Another reason the *Redeye* was so hot was that they were into this new thing all the kids were doing called social media. Twitter had just hatched, and Facebook had just established itself as the new norm. The *Redeye* was right there, interacting with its readers online. I followed their account on Twitter at first because I liked the tone of whoever was behind it. But it wasn't until I got to meet my dreamboat celebrity crush by following their advice that I became an avid fan.

Vince Vaughn was having a premiere for some awful movie located just a few blocks from the Tribune Tower, which was just next door to my work. Sitting on Twitter, I noticed the *Redeye* tweet out the location and time of the premiere. I booked it down the street, was mistaken for a member of the press camera crew because I was standing in the wrong section, and a quick hour later, saw my #1 celebrity crush, Baba Ganoush!

Another genius thing the *Redeye* was doing with their social media was connecting with their readers. I know, right? Communicating to their consumers? Crazy! But they used their social media well, creating a special section on their website reserved for *Redeye* super fans, called *Redeye Royalty*. I was picked in the second round and was given special powers such as writing in the *Redeye Royalty* blog on the paper's website, submitting answers to the sports 5 on 5 question panel that appeared in the paper, and other such luxuries of fame and prestige. The genius behind all this included the person I have deemed as my writing fairy godmother: Steph.

Steph is the coolest person you will ever meet. Why? Because she's Steph. She's like that Dos Equis ad campaign of The Most Interesting Man in the World, but she really does all those things! Here are some things off the top of my head I can think of:

- She moved from Singapore and has lived in more states that I have ever visited.
- She climbed up a really tall mountain with only a rope ladder and nothing to keep her from plummeting.
- She has a super fancy job where she works from home and travels all over the world, AND she gets all her work done.
- She takes hip hop classes.

There's tons more, but this book isn't about Steph and I'm making myself look lame in comparison. Bottom line, Steph made *Redeye Royalty* cool, and in doing so found hidden talent among the royals, including a post by yours truly which led to tons of fun, exciting life moments. And it was perfect timing too- at work, I was drowning in boredom, to the point where I was getting sad. I was miserable on the train coming in to work, staring out the window all sad like, as if I were in a movie and Vince Vaughn just broke up with me. By January I was in a slump and over a few beers at a bacon covered chocolate tasting, I decided to do something crazy and blog about how I wanted to run the Chicago marathon. Considering my lifestyle choices consisted of eating bacon covered chocolate, and having never ran more than a block since high school, usually for the train that I just missed, this was a big, crazy goal. I figured putting it on the internet would hold me accountable, but I had no idea that on the other end of the internet, Steph was waiting to call me out on my bluff and make me do the craziest thing ever.

Two days after I blogged about how I wanted to run the Chicago marathon, Steph sent me an email. It went something like this:

Hey! Saw your blog Monday. Would you really run the marathon? If so we might have a spot for your own *Redeye* blog. Let me know!!!! :)

Which led me to reply something like:

OMG YES I'LL DO ANYTHING TO WRITE FOR YOUR PUBLICATION! AAAHHHHHHHHH!

And then I thought this:

Ohhhhhh crap. I think I have to run for real.

But the opportunity to have lots of readers read my stuff in addition to my original fan base of three was too enticing to say no. Every time I got a tiny sentence in the paper, I was floored, and now I had the chance to have an online column, which would be promoted by the paper, which would be seen by the city, with MY face on it. It was perfect and exactly what I needed to get me out of my bureaucratic slump.

So I was on my way to getting my very own online column about running a marathon, having no previous running or professional writing experience. And that was just the first month of 2010.

The second month of the year is the most important, as it is my birthday month. Yes, month. I am so great that I enjoy extending my birthday festivities as long as possible, well past the inevitable, "Your birthday was two weeks ago! You get a day not a month!" rants that typically come from people who obviously hate me. Yes, February 15th is a day of greatness and consists of much drinking, partying, presents and cake. But this year was different because I was turning 25, an age set aside for quarter-life crises, and in my case, growing pains.

I was sick of living at home. Much like working at IHD, there wasn't anything wrong with it really; it was more me and my anxiousness for the next step in life. My mom cooked me dinner, my dad drove me to work when he was going downtown, my sister and I each had our own room, and there were two working toilets in our dormed-out bungalow. This was any young Chicagoan's ideal living situation, and it came at the low, low price of free. Yet I was restless. I stomped around agitated, like a PMSing brown haired Goldilocks, unpleased with every chair in the house, complaining my home cooked dinner was too hot or too cold. Honestly, my parents should have slapped me, but they didn't, because it was paradise. And I was tired of living in comfort.

By spring I sprung free. I packed up my things and headed north. One mile north to be exact. But it was a different zip code! And I had an apartment all to myself! In charge of buying my own frozen pizza and beer! Even though it took me about a month to officially move everything out, the second I did, I got a phone call from my mother, who screamed the following:

WHEN YOU MOVE OUT OF SOMEONE'S HOUSE, YOU CALL THEM AND TELL THEM!

She was sad her first born baby was flying the nest. Granted, I was so close that she could have somersaulted her way to my new place, but I get it. She was left with the least favorite daughter; I'd be upset too. My dad did not take it as harshly. I don't think he knows I moved out, so don't tell him. He probably thinks I'm in the basement doing my laundry, or upstairs in my room listening to Ricky Martin.

Even though I was settling in nicely with the new place and new writing gig, I still wasn't pleased. I would come into work every morning and stare out the window at the TRIBUNE sign next door. I figured getting a job, any job, inside the building would make things better. Even the building's exteriors showed the difference. IHD's building was brown and drab, with dull windows that had a brownish tint, and nothing exciting when you entered the main lobby. The Tribune tower, on the other hand, was an actual, neo-gothic styled tower with buttresses and gargoyles. The outside exterior has rock fragments of historical places, like the great pyramids in Giza and the Taj Mahal. The best part of the IHD building was the cafeteria station that made a mean buffalo chicken wrap with ranch instead of blue cheese. I had to get in the tower, even if it meant starting from the bottom at a soul-sucking job. I planned to first get in any job I could find, then work my way up to a writing job, per the American way. Actually, I probably just stole that from the movie Confessions of a Shopaholic.

Up until this point, I couldn't network to save my life. If someone said at a mixer, "Go make small talk with that person about marketing or put your head in that guillotine." I would have chosen a beheading instantly. But with the new *Redeye Royalty* group, I was able to squeeze my way in with similar, introverted/talkative people, one of which was able to help me find a job as a sales analyst for one of the Tribune's smaller subsidiaries. When I had the interview, I literally snuck underground to lower Michigan Avenue with my suit jacket, walked down to the next stairway leading to upper Michigan Avenue, and ran inside so that none of my coworkers at IHD could see that I was going in for an interview. Even though it was the same commute for almost the same pay, it felt like a whole new world, and the *Redeye* was my magic carpet ride inside.

After that, things started to snowball into awesomeness. I was on a progressive track to getting out of a dead-end job. Turns out that having goals and dreams and crap turned my life from a sad country song into one of those catchy, upbeat songs you hear during a movie montage where the female protagonist changes things around by buying new clothes and cleaning her apartment. I was doing it all! I was on top of the world! Mary Tyler Moore hat toss in the air with a fist pump!

12a Floors of Anxiety, A Play

(Fun Fact: In most tall buildings, you won't find a '13' button in the elevator. Why? Because people were hella superstitious back in the day.)

CHARACTERS

CONNIE   Beautiful twenty-something-year-old, brown hair, rocking ass, hates everything except cupcakes.

OTHER PEOPLE   Not as relevant, all annoying.

SETTING   The elevator of a 30-floor building in the Loop, downtown Chicago.

TIME   9:23 AM. But if her boss asks, she was there early but had to run out for 'personal items.'

ACT 1

CONNIE: (Steps on the elevator) *Good God, what the hell is that smell?*

(Two older men in their 40s get on the elevator)

CONNIE'S INNER MONOLOGUE: (Makes disgusted look and looks around for smell) *It was not me. It was not me. Fuuuu-what if these people think I am the smelly one? It was not meeeee!!!!*

(One man immediately gets off.)

CONNIE: *Come back, sir! I wasn't the one who shat myself I swear!*

(Elevator door closes.)

CONNIE: [looking constipated, smiles] *Yeah dude, that wasn't me.*

(Elevator door opens. A woman on her phone steps inside.)

WOMAN ON PHONE: "Just tell him we'll eat dinner after the game. Hello? I'm in an elevator; I can't hear you.

CONNIE: (Death stare.)

WOMAN ON PHONE: "Hello? I'M ON AN ELEVATOR. I'LL CALL YOU WHEN I GET OFF. GET OFF! WHEN I-Hello?"

CONNIE: *Get off. Now.*

(Elevator door opens. Five douchebags in their 20s get in, all male.)

BAG 1: "Yeah, Mike thinks he's getting those comps today. He's not."

BAGS 2-5: "Hahahahahaha."

CONNIE: *Eww.*

BAG 4: "What's that smell?" (Looks behind him towards Connie, silent man, and woman who is now rapidly texting.)

CONNIE: *motherf-*

BAG 3: "You going to the happy hour event tomorrow?"

BAG 1: "Ehhhh, Might as well, doesn't hurt to make an appearance. Last time the bartender made it an extra happy hour with some free shots. We got SO wasted. HaHA!"

BAGS 2-5: "Hahahahahaha."

CONNIE: *Hahahahaha. OMG you're so cool bro. Hahahaha. I bet the bartender wants you to be her boyfriend. Douche.*

WOMAN ON PHONE: (holds phone up to see if text message will send in the elevator that has just cut her off.)

CONNIE: (Death stare.)

(Previously quiet man starts sneezing multiple times in a row while barely attempting to cover his mouth with his arm.)

CONNIE: *Ahhhhhhhhh! I am in a petri dish of death!!! Ahhhhhhhh!*

WOMAN ON PHONE: (Woman on phone looks annoyed. Bag 4 turns around yet again.)

CONNIE: *What do you think is going to happen by turning around dude? Can you trigger a defense shield from this smell by turning your neck? Stop looking back here, asshat.*

MAN: (Previously quiet man starts grunting up the rest of the phlegm that isn't splattered across the elevator into his throat.)

CONNIE: *Why did you turn this elevator into a box of boogers? Why??? I hate you I hope you choke on your snot for infecting me with the plague. CURSE YOU AND YOUR ENTIRE SNOT-FILLED FAMILY MAY YOU ALL GET RAW NOSTRILS FROM YOUR DISEASE AND HAVE YOUR EYES FALL OUT.*

(Elevator doors open. Previously quiet man gets off.)

CONNIE: *Rot in Helllllllll!*

(Elevator doors open to Connie's floor).

CONNIE: [Quietly] "Excuse me."

(None of the bags move.)

CONNIE: [Slightly less quiet.] "Excuse ME." (Shoves between two bags of douche, makes sure to swing purse wide enough to hit another.)

CONNIE: *DIE ALL YOU PILES OF FECES! DIE THE FOULEST DEATH POSSIBLE!*

WOMAN WITH PHONE: (Still in the elevator, answers as doors closing.) "Hello?"

CONNIE: (Walks into office floor, sees boss walking down the hall.) "Good morning!"

CONNIE: (Walks into her cubicle. Throws down purse. Looks at clock that says 9:24. Puts head on desk. Dies.)

End scene.

Will Run for Blog

THERE ARE TWO STRATEGIES that I know of to be a sure-fire way to become popular, make friends, and get your picture in the newspaper. One is making a sex tape; the other is running the Chicago marathon. To date, I have only done one, and it worked out nicely.

I started writing as Marathon Missfit in January of 2010, and I actually started running at the beginning of March. Getting started with the *Redeye* was the coolest thing ever. I had my very own blog, with a header that had me lying across the top, exactly like Carrie's picture on the bus in *Sex and the City*, only I was about 80 pounds heavier than Carrie, and I was in sweatpants and gym shoes instead of the naked dress.

Steph and I chose Marathon Missfit because it perfectly captured that I was not by any means an expert, in case people failed to see me lying down on top of a running blog and didn't get the hint already. I had my very own photo shoot for the blog where I picked out a brand new fuchsia hoodie from Target. It was all so glamorous! I was like a celebrity! I even got paid a two-figure monthly salary!

By March I figured I should start running since I had exhausted all my posts about what to wear when trying to run, and why running a marathon sounds hard. I ran my first 5k distance on St. Patrick's day and swore up and down California Avenue, jealous that the rest of the city was downtown watching the river get dyed green while I schlepped my sober ass up and down the street.

Soon after, the parties started, and I had more fun things to do than burn calories. Steph was now hosting *Redeye Royalty* parties monthly, where everyone connected with the *Redeye*, and their readers, could all meet up in real life as opposed to hitting a thumbs up button as their sole form of contact. It was very unconventional, but I was determined to go and meet new people since I hadn't made a new friend since high school. So I did what any sane person does who wants to venture out and meet new people- I grabbed my best friend (named Alicia. See Chapter 2 if you forgot, I'm not writing another description) and dragged her to my first *Redeye* party.

We walked into Faith & Whiskey for the first time, even though it was blocks away from our former college, DePaul. As soon as we entered, you could tell exactly where the *Redeye* crowd was congregating vs. the typical college kid crowd. For one, the *Redeye* patrons were not young kids drinking shitty beer in striped sunglasses and popped pink collars. Also, other than the *Redeye* employees who were naturally outgoing, the rest of the crowd had a look of nervousness about them, as if their mothers made them attend so they would be more socialized in the big city. Thick framed glasses galore, it was a weird combination of feeling uncomfortable that you only knew each other through the internet, yet a feeling of ease that no one looked crazy enough to try and mess with you, and if they did, you could throw their glasses on the ground and run.

I made it a mission to introduce myself to each of the other bloggers who were there that night. Elliot made it easy by introducing himself to me, which I made it easier for him to approach us by bringing my hot Hispanic friend to lure him in (thanks Alicia!). Elliot was the Geek to Me online columnist, and oddly enough, he was the most extroverted one in the room. Say what you want about the geek culture, I'm pretty sure they have the highest track record for getting laid at parties. Possibly higher than college kids getting wasted off of shitty beer.

We talked to Elliot for a bit about his blog, what he did with his readers that worked, and how I too could become a Jedi blogger, if I followed the path of the X-Men when I got the bat signal. Or something like that. I lost interest as soon as he mentioned Star Wars. One beer later, we got down to the standard questions you ask everyone you meet in Chicago:

1. Where are you from?

2. What neighborhood do you live in?

3. What grammar school did you go to?

Somewhere in our conversation, I revealed to him my secret identity of being half-Mexican, and he revealed his Puerto-Ricanness. Then the greatest thing ever happened.

Without blinking an eye, without any reference said beforehand, the two of us in unison began snapping our fingers and circling each other, preparing to fight like the Sharks and Jets in A West Side Story. If I had done that to the puking college kids drinking shitty beer, they would have tried to start fighting me for real. It was then as I was circling my fellow blogger colleague pretending to get into a race war that I knew I was in good company.

Next up was Stephen Markley. A week before I went to the event, I went to one of those custom running shoe stores where they don't let you pick out shoes based on how pretty they look, but rather whether you can run in them without your feet falling off from pain. I got to talking with the sales girl there who, when I told her I was becoming one of the *Redeye* bloggers like so and so, so and so, and Stephen Markley, her exact words were, and I quote, "Stephen Markley? Woah, he's trouble!" When I pried, she simply explained that her friend briefly dated him (drunkenly banged) and changed the subject. But her eyes conveyed that this kid was either some wild lunatic, or one of those *John Tucker Must Die* rip-offs, who gets every girl in the city to date, then hate them.

One look into Stephen Markley's eyes, I realized what led the shoe sales girl to react. He had the bluest freaking eyes in the entire world. They were so blue that I was afraid if I stared into them for too long I would become instantly pregnant. Since I was betrothed, I was immune to his Midwestern charms, but I could totally see why complete strangers would remark on his demeanor, although the poor kid didn't stand a chance with those weapons of mass cuteness.

I said a quick hello to him and expected little conversation. Seeing as I could not offer my purity up as a sacrifice to his ocean blue eyes, I figured we wouldn't have much to talk about other than our writing. But then I remembered what the shoe sales girl said and told him the anecdote, thinking he'd find it amusing. The poor guy seemed surprisingly concerned his name was strewn about the city. I would be too if people were callously bugging their eyes out in a shoe store at the mention of my name. I tried to help solve the mystery of why she mentioned his name in such a way by explaining who she was- average height, thin, brunette, tan, which led us nowhere. After I befuddled him and told the story of how his name was being slandered all over town, we ran out of things to say, but he wished me good luck in my running and I him in his next one night stand.

The last blogger I met was hard to get to, so I thought I would leave without completing my mission until it was time to leave. I was yanking my coat out from a girl in a bright green strapless dress who was deep in conversation with a friend, and when I yanked too hard, she turned around and gave me a death glare. I instantly recognized her as the *Redeye* dating blogger, and mumbled a hello and quick explanation of who I was. She stopped glaring and said hello, and we talked for a minute. Little did I know that night was that sitting on my coat was my soon to be favorite brunch buddy, a woman who could not only drink me under the table but would push me under it for amusement as I chugged Miller Lite to sober up.

Anna was my first writing friend. A transplant from Iowa, she was able to dominate the city effortlessly, and every time we go out for a quick brunch, it soon turns into pitchers of margaritas, nachos for lunch, and gallons of beer for dinner. Women of the earth, I implore you to find a person in your life who can motivate you to find the true potential in your dreams while ordering you another round of mimosas. I'm pretty sure that is one of those habits successful people have that somehow gets cut from those Forbes lists.

It's also a good sign of finding a good friend when you are the best when they are around. Some people realize this when their friends motivate them to do well; I found this to be true with Anna when I kicked her date out my car by swearing like a sailor who has herpes.

It was winter, and we were en route to sing karaoke (another sign you have found a good group of people- if you can sing Disney songs drunk with a person, they'll probably save your life one day). Anna, her date, and Jen, another *Redeye Royal*, were all in my car as we were heading down North Avenue. Traffic was slow, and Jen and I could hear the hushed bickering of the two non-love birds in the back seat. I could smell how un-sober nameless dude (who hadn't introduced himself or shook our hands- a sign of evil) was from the front, but I kept quiet and went over possible set lists with Jen.

Then, at a stop sign, drunk nameless dude decides the free ride to the bar needed to end, slurred a quick I'm outta here, and whipped my door open only to door a bicyclist to the ground.

When one is thrown into chaos, it is important to save oneself before helping others, which is why I proceeded to scream the following in this order.

1. IS MY DOOR OKAY? DID HE DAMAGE MY DOOR?
2. Oh shit, is that biker okay? Oh, he's getting up, That's good.
3. GET THE (BEEP) OUT OF MY MOTHER (BEEP) CAR YOU MOTHER (BEEEEEP).

Drunk dude sat in confusion as my baby (my Rav4) was being examined by Jen for scratches and the bicyclist examined himself for internal bleeding. I proceeded to scream and swear until the drunk guy gained clarity and realized that the woman screaming George Carlin's *7 Words You Can Never Say on Television* were all directed at him. He exited, and I drove off in a rage, taking Anna and Jen hostage and leaving the douche in a situation where, I hope, ended in the bicyclist kicking his ass.

After a few blocks, I calmed down. After a night of drinking and singing songs, Anna was unphased by the drunkard's absence. I was glad she didn't get upset that I helped throw a man out of her life who didn't deserve to be in it. If I could just get a full-time job kicking assholes out of people's lives, I think I'd be pretty successful. Next time someone is in need of break-up assistance, I'll be over, with a bat, ready to take care of business.

After a few of these fabulous parties, I realized I should probably start running for real. The glory of my first 5k had worn off, and I realized maybe I ought to get some miles in before race day. Steph had the smart idea (she has no other kind) to start a running group, which would promote my blog community. I thought this was brilliant and imagined dozens of new runners all being led by me on the lakefront path, dressed like we were in a Nike commercial. I announced a meetup place and time and gave strangers on the internet the option to either come run with me or stalk and murder me, their choice.

That morning I was worried no one would show. Then on the way there, I was afraid they would show. I had no clue what to expect, but in my dozens of scenarios, I always pictured different versions of me-women who were new to running and who didn't want to be awake at the ass crack of dawn. So when two fit men came looking for Marathon Missfit, I was thrown off yet again.

Alec and Jeff were both tall, slender, and looked like they already ran a marathon before breakfast. Compared to my flabby exterior, I was the fatty corned beef in between two pieces of low fiber bread. We started heading out south on the Chicago lakefront path, and I prefaced by saying very clearly if they wanted to break out ahead and meet back (or just run far, far away from me), I was totally fine. Both declined, and we set out for six miles.

Mile one and two were slow and unnerving. It's hard trying to make small talk with strangers, but it's quadrupled in difficulty when you are breathing as if a dinosaur is sitting on your chest. By mile three we hit a nice rhythm- both were talking, and I was trying not to interrupt with my dry heaving and gasping for sweet, delicious air.

A little after mile 4 struck I was done. I told them I needed to walk, and both were gracious enough to stay back with me. I was humiliated, but it was hard to feel like a tool when two nice guys are walking you back to your car. After that Jeff went on to train solo, but Alec agreed to come back with me next week. And that was the day I found my running buddy.

Alec lived in Logan Square- a neighborhood gentrified enough so that nice well to-do gentlemen like himself would buy a condo there and bring up the value of the area. The oldest of four brothers, Alec was the first generation of Polish immigrants and was raised in Minnesota before he moved to Chicago for school to become an architect. If I ever decide to adopt a child, I am going to specifically ask for a child born of Minnesota/Polish parents, because those are the nicest people in the world.

Our Saturday routine went as followed. I would wake up between 4:30-5: 00 AM, eat something with peanut butter on it (I aimed for bread, but it was so freaking early I probably just smeared it on a paper towel for all I know). Then I would drive to Alec's condo and pick him up. Being so early, I was lucky in that there was a Marathon gas station located on the corner of California Avenue that alerted me that it was the corner where I had to turn to pick him up. Alec would come in and always smell like the Snuggle fabric softener. At the time he was single, and all I could think was what a shame it was that this eligible Snuggle the bear smelling bachelor was wasting away his Saturday mornings with me when the thousands of women in Chicago who were drunkenly stumbling home would probably give up their right stiletto to meet a nice guy like him!

We would drive to Montrose harbor where there was always plenty of parking before sunrise, and we would head south on the lakefront path. Alec would run the first few miles with me before breaking out into his tempo pace. I would stay at one pace the entire time- survival pace- slow enough to not die, fast enough to technically be considered running. If you're looking for hard numbers, Alec was running about 8-minute miles, I was somewhere between 11-13 minute miles, not including walking breaks.

Running with Alec was an infinity times more fun than running alone. One can only listen to Britney Spears' "Circus" (my go-to pick me up song) so much before one goes insane. Once I even tried listening to a book I downloaded on iTunes. It was by Jen Lancaster, but I immediately regretted the decision when she went into a detailed description of preparing a succulent pork tenderloin dinner with lots of wine, which made me starving and angry I was up and running instead of sitting and eating pork.

Alec and I had lots of fun running. We would talk about our relationships- me with my betrothed, him with his dating life, and a new lady whom he met. I interpreted his trust to open up about his dating life as a request for unsolicited advice from me, the self-proclaimed expert, so I would often shout things at him such as "Just tell her you love her and marry her already! She sounds nice and she has pretty hair! What's the holdup?" I'd like to think I had everything to do with their marriage that later happened, but in reality, he probably never heard me, as I am a low talker and was always out of breath.

Our favorite thing to do on the running path was to check out the scenery. And by the scenery, we meant the hot pieces of ass running past us on the lake. It's nice having a friend to whom you feel comfortable expressing your preference to shirtless men. I encourage it as a bonding experience with any coworkers with whom you might have a struggle finding a common thread over. Because in the end, everyone likes looking at a runner's body. Amen.

Speaking of running bodies, I was turning into a piece of chiseled rock. Well, my legs anyway. It started out a little strange, when I found a fatty area around my ankles, freaked out, and thought somehow I was running incorrectly and was now forming cankles. To this day I'm not sure what it was, but it eventually went away, and I traded my cankles in for rock-hard calves. Calf muscles are pretty easy to develop, but what made me feel awesome was the line in my thigh. A muscle if you will, which were held captive to my pants and were in dire need of flaunting. By early fall I was rocking jean skirts and leg muscles so well I looked like I could be in a leg muscle/jean skirt commercial.

And the writing was getting good too. I was getting recognized on the train (once), I had comments on my blog (a few), and I was even in the paper (somewhat). Things were going great, until I almost pooped my pants.

The story of how I almost pooped my pants, told everyone, and then was embarrassed by it

Getting a compliment on one's writing is the best thing in the world, unless it pertains to a story where you talk about almost shitting your pants.

By this time in my training, things were moving along well, mainly because I was actually moving. Alec and I were on a weekly long-run schedule, and I was hitting double digits on Saturdays. We were all at the *Redeye* Rooftop party at the Tribune Tower on Michigan when one of the *Redeye* reporters approached me in response to my latest blog entry that came out the day before.

"I loved your blog today! So funny. Yeah...I sometimes have a hard time finding a bathroom too.... (awkward pause)."

Fame and glory should come with a manual. And that manual should have one piece of advice that says, "Do not write a blog entry on not being able to find a bathroom on the lakefront path that is, albeit hilarious, goes into great detail about you needing to take a shit. And don't leave the blog entry open for the reader to think that you may have shit your pants. And, above all else, do not write this entry the day before you go to a fancy rooftop party downtown when you want to look cool." Unfortunately, I did not read the nonexistent manual, so many people at the party came up to talk to me about this.

How did I almost shit my pants? Fine, you twisted my arm. I'll tell! I'll tell!

It was a typical long run morning- pick up Alec, start out slow, break out and keep running south. No big deal. We had gotten to the starting point particularly early that day, so early, in fact, the sun was not out yet. Insane? Yes. But it was necessary to avoid the heat forecasted for the day, plus running in the morning on a Saturday is great because for the rest of the day you can drink beer, sleep, and eat pizza with no judgment because YOU went running that morning.

From Montrose to Fullerton Avenue, the lakefront path goes into a tree-lined area, where you go through a few underpasses, pass the Lincoln Park Zoo, and around some more trees before you hit the open scenery of the lake. I had made it to the beautiful lake right as the sun started to poke out from the water, a scene Alec and I joked that we had seen more times with each other than our significant others. I was distracted from the picturesque scene to my left by a deep, strong churning in my stomach, medically known as the start to runners' shits.

When you run, your stomach bounces up and down, churning the peanut butter paper towel you had for breakfast. I was alone and could see the North Avenue boathouse where bathrooms were located not too far ahead. I set my sight on the destination and went from a brisk run to a butt-clenched jog, to a twisted-leg wobble designed to stop myself from having an accident all over the Lake Michigan beach.

What seemed like an eternity later, I got to the boathouse, only to find out that it was so freaking early, they weren't open yet. Panicked, I envisioned myself having to shit in a bush, or running into the lake to take a dump, but without toilet paper, I was afraid I would just be stuck there, pants down, in a pool of my feces. As I was wobbling along, a city worker was taking a golf cart down the path, and I jumped in front as if my life was in danger. I begged them for help and explained I needed a toilet opened immediately, lest they want to find a pile of human poop on their nice trail. The man looked at me as if he stumbled into yet another drunk/drugged up crazy person, some of which find their way on the path. My guardian angel in a neon vest explained there was an underpass half a mile up that had bathrooms, and I dashed away.

I don't know how, but by the grace of God and my bowels, I made it. Never in my life have I been more relieved that I did not end up shitting my pants, and the rest of the run was a breeze compared to the almost-nightmare that occurred in my pants.

Sitting at the party with the Chicago skyline as my backdrop, I was slightly mortified for being acknowledged for my article. But as much as I wanted to jump off the rooftop every time someone mentioned my "poop story," it made me realize that I finally developed a writing style- self-deprecating humor. My posts were not about how wonderful it was to be a runner, or how great an athlete I was becoming. Instead, the posts I loved to write, and the ones that got the most attention were the ones where I shared the humility in running. The gross/funny/weird things that happen to everyone, but because most are shy (or maybe they have tact), they tend not to share. I had something to work with, and I was more than ready to share it all with the world. Even if it meant pooping myself a little.

By late summer, when runs lasted more than an hour, I was hooked. I was eating, drinking, sleeping running. Was I in love with running? Hell to the no. Running for me was and is a tricky beast. Some days I would bust through a 5 mile run with ease, some days it was hard to make one loop around the park across the street. One time I was at Horner Park for a run, and I sat down and started bawling like a baby. Don't know why, just did. I cried and cried and cried, then stomped home and cried some more. Some would detect PMS was at hand, but I assure you, it was the emotional toll running took on me. Training for a long distance race is grueling, and on that park bench, I got why people say running is mostly mental, because you have to be a little mental to commit to running 26.2 miles.

It was all worth it though because marathon weekend was the greatest day of my life. I was brought on WGN radio to talk about how I felt pre-race. Then I went to the expo with Alec where we loaded up on free stuff, found our names on the Nike marathon wall of fame, and I took a picture with Ryan Hall, famous runner dude (or Olympian, if you want to get technical). We ended the evening by carb loading in Little Italy, a very peaceful night before one of the biggest day of our lives.

The entire race was a dream- the first half whizzed by, the best part being Boystown, where I was so grateful for the LGBT community who had the most excited crowds to see us runners on the course. The second half was filled with neighborhoods I have never been to before, despite having lived in the city my entire life. I never hit the infamous wall- a mental block runners sometimes face during marathons, but at one point I was weirdly annoyed with my sunglasses, threw them off, and regretted it the rest of the course. But by the end I was in disbelief that I had finished, so spectators at the finish line saw me stumbling around slurring, "Is this it? Is this it?" because I couldn't believe I was at the finish line.

Being raised Catholic, I had the pleasure of imagining what heaven was like my entire life. Now, I think it is like finishing a marathon. After what felt like an eternity, I wandered into the spectator grounds where you find your family and friends. There in my own little section was everyone I knew- my parents and sister, my betrothed, his family, and all my friends. This is exactly what I imagine heaven to be like- reuniting with all the people in your life who made running 26.2 miles worth it. That, but with fewer leg cramps.

I had a job the year I was running the marathon, but it was insignificant compared to what I accomplished that year. New friends, new life goal accomplished, and a new understanding that I could do anything I set my mind to if I simply got up off the couch. Crying on park benches, waking up at the ass crack of dawn, and muscle pain that made it difficult walking up stairs was all worth it for what I gained.

That and the fact that I got to eat whatever I wanted guilt-free for like eight years.

Six Month Review

We are well into the halfway point of this book, which is awesome on so many levels. If this were a job, which at some points in writing it sure feels like it, this would be the time where you, the manager, would call me into your office for a mid-year check-in, just to, 'get a feel for how things are going.' This meeting serves a purpose not only to subtly tell me what I am doing wrong but also to light a fire under my butt in case I am slacking. Let's begin, shall we?

How are you settling in here?

Pretty well! I think it took some adjustment at first; I spent the first few months writing only two chapters and walking around like I was F. Scott Fitzgerald. But then my ego subsided and brought me back to reality so I could hunker down and get to this point. I can't believe we are already midway through. This is great!

Have you settled into your routine here as the author of the book?

(This is where I would look at my hands quizzically while I try to make up some bullshit.) I think so. I've narrowed down the rest of the chapters that need to get written, and I spend loads of time on Twitter scrolling through the #amwriting hashtag for inspiration. Then I get something to drink and watch *Gilmore Girls* with Chompers for a good half a day, and then if I'm lucky, I write a chapter.

Yes, I've been meaning to say something about that. You might want to stop referencing your *Gilmore Girls* watching; I think you've hit your limit.

Really? So soon? Oh, ok then. Can I still talk about Twilight?

It's a little outdated. How about 50 Shades of Grey?

Absolutely not. I read one paragraph of that garbage and it made me weep for the writing world. I'll cut back on the TV rerun references, no worries.

Good. And if you could maybe explain how you are not as lazy of a drunken slob as you make it seem. Perhaps talk about your writing process?

Can do, boss.

Excellent. Now get out of my office, you've got work to do.

Then I would stand around awkwardly, unsure of whether I should shake your hand or not before finally leaving.

Poop Stories of Love

ONE OF THE BEST GIGS I ever signed up for was an ad I found in a paper from a guy in search of a wife.

It was early June, and I was in the midst of my two-week notice from working for the state to working for the Tribune. At 25, I was just starting to settle into my first apartment. And my brand new love of my life, Chompers, the part black Lab, part Great Dane, part horse who I rescued a week before to serve as protection was settling in nicely by claiming my new sofa sectional as his bed. My apartment was a single bedroom unit on the third floor of a courtyard apartment building on Western Avenue, right by Welles Park in Lincoln Square, which is known for its quaintness and small-town feel despite being located in the city. I had a short commute to the Brown line which took me just a few blocks away from both the new job and the one I was leaving behind.

Because I had less than two weeks left (and because I was working for the state), I was taking my sweet time going to work in the morning. Andrew, my boyfriend of ten years, texted the night before to say he was staying late at his parents that night and probably wouldn't be back, which was fine. I was up that night anyway with my mom, who was particularly, and had this weird tone to her voice as if I was dying of tuberculosis and she was calling to send me her love. Little did I know she was just excited that I was going to get engaged the next day.

As I got out of the shower that morning to get dressed for work, I saw a text from my boss Laura with the words, 'OH MY GOD THE *REDEYE*!!!' I thought this was odd since I didn't have anything scheduled to be put in print that day. Luckily she sent this because, in total honesty, if I knew my article wasn't going to be in the paper, my readership went down slightly depending on how late I was for the train. Most likely I wouldn't have stopped at all if she didn't send that text. Intrigued, I made a note to stop at the newspaper box outside the train station entrance before I headed in for work. I slipped on my gym shoes, which paired horribly with my somewhat decent black skirt and grey t-shirt combo, and started out the door.

I grabbed one of the last copies out of the red painted newsstand and skimmed through. Since the spot where I typically had bylines was on page 4, I flipped there first. Nothing. I then skimmed through looking for the 5 on 5, a panel of five writers who were asked five sports questions and would provide funny responses. I was occasionally gifted a spot despite knowing nothing about sports except for the trash talking part. One of the first questions I answered for the 5 on 5 was 'How will the Bulls cope without Tyrus Thomas for a month?' to which I replied (not having a clue who Thomas was) 'Maybe they can borrow some of the Bears players;

they aren't doing anything this season.' (Because the Bears sucked that season). Ba dum-bum-CSSHH!

I flipped open to the sports section, only to see not me, but Andrew's face in one of the slots. His unrelated answers to the sports questions were as follows.

1. I love you Connie.
2. Will you marry me?
3. I will be outside your office awaiting your response.
4. If you say yes, I won't make you watch the NBA finals in the future.
5. But, we still have to go to the Irish Bistro to watch the U.S. win [some soccer game]. That is my one condition.

It turns out he had asked my editors if he could propose in the paper when we were at a *Redeye* event. That was before he took my parents and Caitlyn to the Irish Bistro, our usual weekend hangout that had the best beers and a bartender who never let us leave with a full bill. There, at the place we often found ourselves each weekend, he showed my parents a ring and asked if he could give it to me. The ring is the size of a small child, and I now call it my ten-year retirement gift from dating.

Yes, you read that right. I dated Andrew for ten years before he put a ring on it. Why so long you ask? Well, if we do the math, ten years subtracted from 25 would be 15- the age I was when I first agreed to go to a homecoming dance at an all-boys school with a guy I didn't know, because Alicia made me.

Sophomore year of high school started out a bit sluggish. I was old enough to run around the city until

10 PM, which magically turned into much later when I stayed over at Alicia's because her mom was cooler with curfew than my mom. October was homecoming season, and since I had zero prospective gentlemen callers, I skipped our all-girls high school dance and opted for a night that involved less prep. But Alicia was scheming to go to St. Patrick's high school dance to hang out with the guy she was into, and in order to do so, she needed to get a date for a guy in her group who was searching for a female to take. Enter Connie, escort to the stars!

I protested just enough to keep up appearances, but knowing damn well I had nothing better to do I obliged when we met with Andrew, and he was forced by his friends to ask me. So our homecoming night would be our first night out. We wore cute outfits and I put glitter blush on my face. Andrew picked me up at Alicia's, and within the first five minutes mentioned that he didn't like social functions. I pulled Alicia into her bathroom under the guise of helping me with my eyeliner and told her I didn't like this guy and didn't want to go.

We got to the dance at a respectable 7 PM, and from there we sat. Not being much of a dancer, Andrew used his other talents to woo me, like talking about politics and history. I was just thrilled to have a senior talking to me I feigned interest and tried to think of any facts from my history classes, which was about as vast as reciting how many world wars the U.S. has entered. That's the other big high school drama piece to this story- we told Andrew that I was a junior so that he would go out with me, a lowly sophomore. He said he figured it out when I was talking to all the sophomores at our table instead of the juniors. He was a smart guy from the beginning.

Another thing Andrew had going for him was his looks. Italian on both sides of the family, Andrew's dark brown hair match his dark brown dreamy eyes that smile when he talks about poop jokes or making fun of Chompers. At 18 he could grow a full beard in three days and had a consistent five o'clock shadow that refused to leave his face even though the boys at St. Pat's had to be cleanly shaven. His strong man muscle arms match his insanely strong calf muscles that he earned from conditioning in high school soccer, which haven't faded with age to this day (thank you, Jesus). So despite the fact that he hated social functions, I was totally OK being seen with him in public.

By the time we left the dance to go to dinner, I was infatuated with him. We had spent most of the dance talking about everything two high school kids could-music, friends, school, and family. Andrew eventually loosened up and danced one slow song with me, which is about the same amount of dancing he later did at our wedding. I pulled Alicia into the bathroom at the restaurant, again feigning eye makeup disaster, and told her we had to come clean about my age because I liked him. She arranged to have it done, and when I confronted him, he brushed it off as if age didn't matter, which it totally does unless you really like the person.

Because I was originally scheduled to go out with our friends to hang out in the woods somewhere (because that's what you do when your parents give you an extra hour of curfew for a dance), Alicia and I headed out after dinner. But not before Andrew and I exchanged phone numbers, and I bravely kissed him on the cheek. I was warned that he probably wouldn't call on account of his shyness. But I knew better and awaited his call the next day, which he made, along with a promise from me to call the day after.

Two painfully long days I had still not called. I was racked with the flu (possibly contracted from sitting outside in the woods in a homecoming dress in October?) and was on my deathbed. But I rebounded willingly, solely on the account that I wasn't going to die without having had a serious boyfriend first. Andrew played it cool and acted as if he wasn't counting the hours awaiting my call, but years later he confessed he had been lying in bed, thinking that that was it and that I would never call when he heard the phone ring followed by his mom shouting his name up the stairs.

This was an event in itself. Every person who lived during the time of a landline knows that there is nothing more terrifying than having a parent pick up when you are calling your crush. An older sibling is equally as terrifying. What you are hoping for is a younger sibling who is too clueless to understand that you, a female, are calling to speak to their brother, a male, and all the *Dawson's Creek* sexual implications it contained. I was not as fortunate and had my mother-in-law who asked me to clarify in disbelief when I said yes, I do in fact want to speak to her son. She then went on a five-minute conversation explaining that he was probably in bed, because ever since he was little, he would fall asleep at nine on the dot, and proceeded to tell me the places she would find him asleep as she called up the stairs to Andrew. As she talked, I stayed in a perpetual stance of a teeth-baring grin, hoping she could sense that I was smiling, and not some rude girl who couldn't look nice when talking on the phone. As terrified as I was to call a boy and be talking to his mother, she put me at ease with her uninterrupted conversation and unknotted my stomach enough for me to inhale and prepare for my first hello to the eldest male son of the house.

Things escalated quickly from there. No, I didn't run the bases. Andrew was too much of a gentleman for that. We did, however, have our first non-school dance date and our first kiss on the same night, thanks to me.

The night started out early with Andrew picking me up in his parents' minivan, blasting Jimi Hendrix down my block in a Black Sabbath t-shirt. I told my mom we were going to a carnival with Alicia, when really we were going to watch the Exorcist. (Sidenote: there are a lot of references in this paragraph that might be throwing off your perception of time. To clarify, it was October, 2000. Andrew liked classic rock music, and the Exorcist was re-released in theaters for its anniversary re-digitalized edition. Cher and Madonna were also making comebacks, but that happens every five years, so that doesn't help much. Some things unique to the year 2000- the song "Say My Name" by Destiny's Child was on the Billboard charts, Tina Fey and Jimmy Fallon were the Weekend Update hosts on SNL, and Bill Clinton was serving his last year in office. Hope that clears things up.)

We headed out, and about an hour later of driving, Andrew confessed he was lost, which was foreshadowing for the future of how I would be the navigating North Star in his life of confusion and uncertainty. Or, that he sucks at directions and I needed to get handy with a map. It was the second.

Once we finally found the theater I was already going to be late for curfew if we were going to sit through all of Reagan turning her head around. Luckily and embarrassingly, I couldn't even get in to see the movie because I wasn't 17 and could not buy an R rated ticket without a parent. I imagine this is the reverse of what old men who date women their kids' age feel like when bartenders ask if their date is their daughter by accident. We got back in the car and drove around some more, looking for a place to eat before we settled on Luke's, a hot dog place because it's hard to think of a restaurant when you're 17 and the only places you go to are with your parents. We were about to call it a night until I spotted a park and demanded to be taken to the swing set, which is the high school version of asking to see a guy's apartment. Andrew obliged and mustered up the courage to kiss me in between talking about Black Sabbath lyrics and asking me what my favorite things were. It was cute ok? Shut up.

In that same month we 'officially' became boyfriend and girlfriend, and before the end of the year we both said I love you. Let's take a moment to recap here at how awesome I am at landing a guy, and how you can to!:

1. Say 'Yes' to a blind date- even if the guy says he hates going out and looks like he is having a miserable time, chances are he is lying and he's going to fall in love with you.
2. Lie about your age- I strongly suggest this if you are in a bind. Just come clean later if you like him. If you don't like him, make up more lies.
3. Kiss him on the first date- Just do it. It's not like you're putting out. Unless you already did that.

4. Don't call him back right away- There are great debates on this that I'm sure opposing sides would argue strongly, but just chill out and don't break your back to call right away if you're not ready. Plus his mom might pick up so you'll need a day to prepare nice things to say. (Although if you are reading this, chances are you are an adult and therefore if his mom does answer, that means he lives at home and maybe just hang up.)

5. Seek opportunities to make out- Most urban cities are filled with public parks. Go to one and kiss each other. It's fun!

6. Be yourself and find out if you like them.- I'm not saying to go make out with anyone you see in a public park, but talk to them for a bit and get to know each other first. Thennnn make out in a park.

So yes, even though I have yet to find a job I am comfortable staying with for multiple years, I was able to find my future husband at the ripe old age of 15. In the past 15 years it hasn't been all fun dates and makeout sessions- some of it was a lot of hard work. One day you can flip out because the other person left used Kleenexes all over the kitchen counter. But then later that week they'll be vacuuming the dog hair without you asking, and you'll fall in love with them all over again. Relationships are like that- hard, dirty work one minute and butterflies and ice cream cones the next. And now that we are married it is intensified because unlike when you are single you can't leave and stomp home. I've tried. But all my underwear is at our house, so I eventually have to come back and face things. One time, Andrew and I were watching TV and a commercial came on asking couples what sport marriage was like. Before we could hear the replies of the couples, I answered back, "a caged death match!" to which Andrew laughed in response- something he rarely does at my cheesy jokes. I always get mad at Andrew because he NEVER laughs at my lame jokes. I feel like I have some real gems sometimes when we're sitting on the couch, but his laugh reaction isn't as strong as most people, so he makes me work for it. But he got it because it IS like a caged match. Although instead of pummeling each other to the death, we try and avoid any mishaps. I want to put a sign up like they do in dangerous work environments in our house that reads, "We have had ___ days without an incident."

Hazard site signs are not the only imagery related to both relationships and work. Marriage itself is like one long job interview in where you are trying to find out if you and your coworker would be a good fit together and work well with each other. During our engagement, there was a time when I realized that even when things got shitty, Andrew was the person I would like by my side. Coincidentally, it was when our walls were literally covered in shit.

We were out at night over the week between Christmas and New Year's visiting friends and had stayed out later than usual. It was snowing out, so by the time we got home we were exhausted from being out and the long drive home. There, in the Western Avenue apartment, was Chompers, who typically sat happily in his cage when we were out but was standing and whining as soon as we opened the front door. We could smell it as soon as we entered- something foul had happened. When we walked in the kitchen, we saw it- Chompers was sick. Not all of him- just his butt. He was standing in what looked like a gorilla cage of explosive diarrhea, wagging his tail worriedly that we would be mad that the cage, himself, and the walls behind the cage were all painted in poop.

Instantly, Andrew and I tag-teamed the situation. He let me deal with Chompers while he attempted to clean out the gorilla cage, which required getting on all fours and crawling into the cage of poop. I was amazed that he didn't cry- a weaker man would have wept at the idea of having to clean out a man-sized box of feces, but not Andrew. After I cleaned up Chompers (who was fine by the way, he kept trying to get us to feed him because apparently sharting all night makes a dog hungry), I watched from a distance, handing Andrew clean-up wipes and being thankful he was there to take care of the mess. That's what you want in a partner and a coworker- someone to help clean up piles of shit with you.

Lastly, you want to be with someone, that when you are feeling your worst, they won't abandon you and will help take care of you. That happened our first New Year's Eve as a married couple, where I spent the entire night puking my life away.

Andrew and I had made plans to go to dinner with my dad (my mom was out with her girlfriends for an early dinner celebration) to a German restaurant in Lincoln Square. The appeal was that the restaurant is known for having the giant boot-shaped beer steins that you could drink merrily as you feasted on heavy wintery German food. We headed out for an early dinner, then planned to go to our friends' for New Year's Eve parties. We picked up my dad at seven and headed for the restaurant. But halfway from the house to the restaurant, I felt sick. It was instantaneous- like a wizard gave me a flu spell, and I was instantly nauseous. By the time we reached the restaurant, I threw my dad and Andrew out of the car, sped back to my parents' house, and just made it to the bathroom for the first puke of the night. As bad as it was, the timing was a good thing- because as much as it sucks having the stomach flu, I cannot imagine what it would be like to have the stomach flu after just eating a heavy German dinner. Blech. I settled in front of the TV and started the rounds of walking back and forth to the bathroom to puke my life away.

I was on the couch still hours later when my dad and Andrew walked/stumbled into the house. On her way home, my mom picked them up. She had to roll the windows down on account of the strong beer smell fuming from the men next to her, followed by a hearty rendition of the oldies song "The Weight" by a band called The Band, which Andrew and my dad loudly sang, while I was home dying.

Out of all the stomach bugs I had as a kid and adult, this one was one of the worst. Clutching my Gatorade that I couldn't even keep down, I gave Andrew my blessing that he could go on and ring in the New Year without me since I most likely would be dead by morning anyway. He said he'd think about it and told me to go to sleep and to try and stop puking. I woke up a few hours later to see a sleeping Andrew, sitting upright next to me and my bucket. My mom later told me that he was worried all night and asked her if he should take me to the hospital, insisting that it wasn't normal for any human to puke this much. Out of all the New Year's Eve's we've spent together, that one was my favorite because Andrew chose me over champagne.

You would think after 15 years I would have more stories about bowel movements from our relationship, but sadly these are the only ones that come to mind. Hopefully, in the years to come, we will have more stories of love and happiness, and a lot less dog diarrhea.

Death and the CTA

I KNOW HOW I'm going to die.

Ok. I have a rough idea of the vicinity and tone in which I will die. It will be commuting related and through some series of embarrassment and frustration that will cause me to collapse and die on the train. I'm fairly confident this is the way I will go for two reasons: 1. I spend most of my time commuting to and from work. 2. There are far too many ridiculously annoying things that could go wrong on said commute, causing me to want to die from humiliation.

If you've never taken the Chicago Transit Authority's train line system, then two things are concrete: 1. You never sat in something wet and hoped that it was just someone's sweat on a seat. 2. You probably call it the Chicago Transit Authority instead of the CTA, the L, or most commonly, the train, as most Chicagoans refer to it. The CTA takes you from the heart of downtown's Loop (because it goes in a loop in the center, or more accurately, a rounded out rectangle) and travels both under and above ground, depending which line you take. Here's a list of the trains:

Chicago Transit Authority 'L' Trains

- Green Line- Goes through some bad neighborhoods. I've never been on it, so I can't talk about it too much.
- Red Line-An underground line of stink. It's always dripping underground, of what, I don't ever want to know.
- Orange Line-Takes you to Midway airport, which takes you to Southwest Airlines, which takes you to places like Florida, so that's nice.
- Brown Line-The main perk of this one is that it's not underground with the mole people like the rest of the lines.
- ·Blue Line-The only line that makes me motion sick because it goes under and above ground. Also the line closest to my house.
- Yellow Line-Some rich person in the suburb of Skokie one day decided they wanted to ride the train, and then this line was created.
- Pink Line-A newer line that no one is sure how to use.
- Purple Line- NOT TO BE TRUSTED. It's a backward version of the Brown line but follows the Red Line path? I don't know. It's confusing.

In my time going to school and working downtown, I have taken the Brown, Red, and Blue line (and the evil Purple once by mistake). The Blue line is a goddamn magic carpet ride compared to the grossness of the Red. In my last job, I would take the Blue line from the beginning of the route near O'Hare airport to the loop. Even though it is only 13 miles door to door, it takes a full hour traveling via train. That's 10 hours a week spent sitting in one of the CTA train cars, crammed next to people who are unfamiliar with the product called deodorant. For a time reference, the Godfather Part II is 3.3 hours. I could almost watch the Godfather II three times each week in the time it takes me to get to work. That's some bull.

It wouldn't be so bad if it weren't for the train people. Although most of the citizens of Chicago who work downtown commute via the CTA, so do all of the random-ass smelly people who are just plain assholes (who are going to get a verbal purse thrown to the face right now). These are the people who take up two seats in rush hour with a backpack, eat greasy meals in a crowded, non-ventilated train car, reek of alcohol at eight in the morning, or perform random acts of hygiene duties during their commute. With all of this stress to see, hear and smell an hour before I start my workday, you can see why the likelihood of me succumbing to my timely demise could very well be sitting next to a stranger clipping their toenails while we wait for the train ahead to move.

Here is an example of the story of how my death could go down.

It was a dark and stormy night…

…which is why it was muggy as hell in the city the next day. It is Monday morning in July, and I am late for a 9:30 AM meeting. I curse my coworkers out for scheduling a morning meeting as I struggle to pull up the only pair of pantyhose I can find. Why pantyhose when it is 90 degrees out? Because my legs were the color of ripe tomatoes from being outside for 10 minutes sans sunscreen that Saturday and I needed to dull the color. I hike up my tights and throw on a black knee-length skirt with a bright Kelly green top. I grab my discounted Ann Taylor suit jacket that I bought when I first started working which for some reason has shoulder pads in it even though I bought it in 2004. I tie my gym shoes, and a quick 43 minutes later I'm out the door ready to take on the world, hopefully with time for coffee beforehand.

Half a block into my one mile walk to the train, I notice two things: my skirt shrunk in the wash and my tights waistline is saggy. This is what I get for buying all of my clothes at Target and not taking clothes out of the dryer. By the end of the block, I have to fix my skirt to readjust the back slit that has twisted its way over to the front side. My tights are sagging at the knees, but I am still able to walk in them. I march on, dripping of sweat before I feel the waistline of my tights sag lower and lower. Past my belly button, past my ass crack, sagging lower and lower, as if they are trying to fall completely into my Nikes.

Luckily, the rows of bungalows I pass to get to the train are quiet, and there are few people on the street. I glance back, check for bystanders, and hike up my tights while rearranging my skirt for the second time. Halfway to the train, I am now walking using only the lower half of my legs, clenching my knees and thighs together to avoid more slippage. It is hot, and I am starting to sweat drips of sweat down my back, undoubtedly leaving a sweat mark located where a tramp stamp would be had I chosen a different path in life.

I waddle into to the train terminal and am thrust to a halt as my CTA Ventra train fare card is having an issue. I go to the pay center, press ten different buttons to reveal that I do have money still left on my card, and proceed to try again. Three swipes later and one annoyed look to a CTA employee sitting in their air-conditioned vestibule, I finally tilt my card the perfect 47 degrees to the left for the card to read properly. I quick-walk down the escalator and proceed to stand for 11 minutes. My hair is frizzed to the max on account of the humidity; some might wonder whether I am heading to work or back to the future.

A man walks in front of me as the train rolls in, yet I push past him to claim a preferred seat in the middle of the train car, away from the doors that waft in hot air every time they open. Ideally, I would be in a window seat, but those are usually taken before my train stop. I manage to get a seat next to a man who appears to have taken a shower this week. I start to readjust everything below my stomach as discreetly as possible. In the walk down the escalator, my tights have managed to take my underwear as a hostage, and have proceeded to pull everything down mid-ass. I wiggle in my seat, and the next two train cars of people avoid me as I look as though I have crabs and am adjusting myself to scratch. By the third stop, I am at a place where I feel as though my derriere is well protected, and I stop to take a look out the window. That is when I hear the noises.

The first sound I hear is crunching. There is a teenage girl with a black polo shirt with an emblem of a charter school stitched on who is sitting ahead of me near the door. She is eating a healthy, well-balanced breakfast of Flaming Hot Cheetos and Pepsi. Directly to my left, there is a thirty-something-year-old, well-dressed man slurping his coffee and 'Ahhhh-ing' after every sip. Slurp, gulp, AHHHH. Slurp, gulp, AHHHH. It's like he's in a god damned Diet Coke commercial. The noises trigger my misophonia (Which is a real thing, I swear. It's something with the wires in your brain and ears that make you sensitive to chewing and other random noises. Symptoms? Enraged anger. Cure? Mentally punching people in the throat.) and I am near kicking the coffee guy in the face when I realize I have headphones in my purse. I crank up my favorite playlist filled with outdated pop hits from the early 2000s, peppered with a few Taylor Swift songs and whatever new song the kids are listening to this day.

I ease into my songs when I glance forward and notice a stench wafting up my nostrils, only to see a man sweating as if he were seated on the sun. Most people on this train are perspiring to some extent, myself included, but most of us have managed to take the proper precautions to avoid smelling like death. This man did not have the time in his morning routine. The scent takes me to another place. An old town in Europe perhaps, where the townspeople don't wear deodorant, or India, where I hear it smells awful in some parts. I put my suit jacket up to my nose and act as if I'm in need of comfort by a soft object instead of filtering out the smell because it's impolite to make someone think you are going to pass out from the smell coming from their body, even if it's true.

By the time I find a comfortable position where my purse handle is safely wrapped around my arm to avoid purse-snatching (mama didn't raise no fool) we are passing stop 10 out of the 17 that make up my commute. We are underground now, nearer downtown, and the train car is at maximum capacity. Another 30-

something, well-dressed man enters, hovering over me. Actually, his large man purse is hovering over me. Whatever jackass made it cool for men to have 'day bags,' or murses (man purses), is a moron. The men I have come across via public transportation have no concept that a purse is an extension of themselves the way women do, and therefore have no control over the large object swinging from their arm, leaving bystanders at its mercy. This man is not removed from this phenomenon, and his man purse proceeds to whack me in the face three times before I give him the death stare that communicates, "Stop hitting me in the face with your lady bag, dude." He gives a half turn, but I am still in the swinging trajectory of the bag holding his sweaty gym clothes and sandwich.

I crank up a set of NSYNC hits and wait for the great exile at Clark and Lake, where 80% of the passengers will exit to transfer to other trains, and I will have enough room to un-scrunch my arms away from my body so that I am not folded like an accordion. Five stops to go and the herd of cattle exit while a crazy man with dreadlocks and scribbled signs steps on the train. I know this man from past car rides, and normally can avoid his presence when I am not running late, which means somewhere between the Cheetos and punching bag, the train is delayed, and I am now late. I glance at my watch and see that I have to bolt as soon as I get to my stop.

The crazy man proceeds to go into his rant like clockwork. He has a speech prepared that he recites each time, which I have nearly memorized on account of my constant lateness. His schpeal is that we are all serving the man and giving him our money. We can walk away from this by choosing our own path (apparently a path to be a crazy train person like he did). Then he goes into something about prostitution and not letting anybody take our body, blah blah blah. Normally he is harmless, so I take my usual stance when near crazy- I pretend I am invisible and make as little movement as possible. This also works in the office when a boss or higher up person comes down the hallway with the look of starting a new project on their face.

Crazy man is getting a little too crazy this day, so instead of waiting for the train to come to a complete stop at my exit, I start to get up and walk toward the exit doors so I can leap out in a hurry. However, as I walk past the seat once vacated by the sweat monster, the train jerks to a halted stop and I fling into the sweaty chair, sitting in something that is definitely not sweat. Mortified, I leap up in horror, causing my tights to lose what little control they had. I make peace with the chair, telling myself it must be water, and bolt out the door.

Using my Nikes for what the mass producers of the footwear intended I sprint up the stairs, opting out of taking the escalator which people refuse to walk up. A Ke$ha song starts up, and I am pumping my leg muscles up each stair as it is my only cardio for the day except when I walk down the block to Potbelly's for my lunchtime ritual of a turkey sandwich and large pop. I get past the first set of stairs, and push through the CTA turnstile, only to have my headphones yanked off my head, the cord tangled around the turnstile bar thingy (there is no word for that thing). I untangle myself and head up the second half of the 77 steps that will take me above ground.

I look up to the top of the stairs, and a beam of sunlight hits me in the face. I pull out my sunglasses and look up again to the sky. At this moment, a pigeon is descending the stairway as they often do because an underground tunnel is cozy to a bird known for disease and garbage eating. This pigeon is a beast though and is extending his wings full-spanned, just like Batman. I look up to see this bird beast flying towards my head, and have the logical reaction of screaming and throwing my hands in the air just as Ke$ha breaks out into the chorus of "Tik Tok," telling me not to stop and make it pop. But my headphones once again gets tangled around me and in the tornado of diseased bird/panty hose dropping/pop singer singing/headphone cord tangling/underworked lack of cardio thighs burning, I lose my balance and fall down the flight of stairs. I am lying on a filthy CTA floor, my tights fallen at the knees, my skirt completely above my waist. Miraculously I do not die as my head lands fortuitously on a pile of used newspapers. However, a coworker passes by and sees my ass exposed, and I die immediately from embarrassment.

A coroner is brought in but not before a few of my other coworkers pass by and see my butt. Since only the Batman pigeon was in the stairway with me, they are left to determine my death by bringing in a Dexter-like type who is astute at determining how I passed on.

The final autopsy reads as follows.

Victim: Connie O'Reyes

Cause of Death: Leaping down CTA stairs in an attempt to twerk.

Details: The victim was clearly insane before the time of death. This is evidenced by the fact that she was dressed in a costume that can be described as Melanie Griffith's famous cinema role in *Working Girl* complete with frizzy hair and shoulder pads in her suit jacket. To make matters worse, she was deeply obsessed with the late 90s, early 2000s as evidenced by her Spotify playlist she was listening to at the time of death. Songs included TLC's *Creep*, Mariah Carey's *Fantasy*, *Poison* by Bell Biv Devoe, and a slew of Biggie, Puff and Mase songs, including *Mo Money, Mo Problems*. The song that the deceased was listening to at the time of death was *We Can't Stop* by Miley Cyrus. Since Ms. O'Reyes' skirt was shifted in such a way that the back slit was in the front between her legs and her panty hose and underpants were at mid-calf level, one can assume she was attempting to twerk and became frustrated causing her to throw herself off the stairs. Her misophonia levels are through the roof, and yes, that is totally a real thing. Judging by her brain waves, she went through a severe series of ill-sounding noises, possibly causing her to feel the need to find an emotional outlet, hence the twerking. A pigeon feather was caught in her hair, and it appears as though she urinated herself as the seat of her skirt is wet, further proving she was mentally unstable at the time of the incident.

Update: A gentleman came up to the scene after examination and said he frequently rode on the same train as the victim. He explained she was a prostitute and explained how he warned her not to let people take her body. This witness seems legit and we are changing the cause of death from bad twerking to a possible *prostitute-related disturbance. Still uncertain why she was wearing pantyhose in July. That's just plain weird.*

And that's how I will most likely die on my way to work and also how my parents will have the unfortunate incident of thinking their perished daughter was a downtown prostitute who rode the CTA.

A Note on Dying

Now that I am theoretically dead in this chapter, I am now contemplating how I got here. We all know the pigeon did it, but why the hell am I writing about my death, and why do I constantly think of how I am going to fall down the subway stairs and plummet to my death in the first place? I have two theories.

Growing up half Irish, my social life throughout my adolescence revolved largely around going to wakes. And not just family (although we did have lots of people die in my family, which is sad, but not the point), being Irish, my mom felt it was her moral obligation to drag us to every person's wake that she knew through a seven degrees of mom. The mailman's wife died? Put your tights on; we're heading over to Cooney funeral home. The ninety-year-old bagger at the Jewel died last week, and we missed the funeral? We'll send a card. Half my weekends as a kid were spent sitting around with my dad and sister in the basement of funeral homes in what I knew it to be as the fun room. To this day, I have spent more hours in the fun room of Cooney funeral home than I have at *Chuck-E-Cheese*. This is the room where there is coffee and water at the very least. At the good places, the funeral directors put out Maurice Lenell cookies, a Chicago cookie company and break room staple at most wakes. You would think that I would have developed some sad association with sweets and be super healthy now, but I am not. That's because it is impossible to be sad when you're eating a Maurice Lenell Pinwheel swirl, a chocolate/vanilla swirl cookie whimsically decorated with a pink sugar coating around the edge. Give me a wake with some pinwheel cookies and free pop, and you've got yourself a party! Never mind the deceased relative lying upstairs, clearly he or she would have wanted you to be happy and feast on stale cookies in memoriam. RIP.

The food and free pop portion of the wake is only one side of what it's like going to an Irish wake. The other is the rambunctious part that involves drinking, singing old Irish songs, and simply getting past the sad event that occurred by sharing good stories to cope and move on.

The whole mysticism of people drinking and laughing with a dead body in the room sounds deliriously pleasant, which is probably why, when asked to draw my tombstone in a grammar school reading project in the third grade, I drew a statue of a giant smile.

Let's take a second to recognize that in third grade I was asked to draw my own tombstone. Umm, what the hell? What kind of crazy people were running Immaculate Heart of Mary grammar school? I'll tell you who- the Catholics. Only in a Catholic school will you find a more concentrated interest in death than at an Irish wake. Between our Savior giving himself up to save our souls, basically all of the saints being killed crazy-style in some sick and twisted way that makes Stephen King sound tame, and apparently mandatory tombstone drawing assignments, it's amazing us Catholics aren't all crazy (save your opinions- although that was a fantastic set up for a joke this isn't that kind of book.)

Back to discussing my wake. When I die, I would like to have the traditional Irish wake. Lots of drinking is a must. Preferably, I would like to have someone make a Connie Cocktail specifically for my day, but other types of booze, mainly beer, should also be present. Next, I'd like my horrible work commute playlist to run on a continuous loop. Once I'm dead, I won't care that everyone knows I listened to old NSYNC songs way more than any adult woman ever should. Maybe a 90s dance battle will ensue, who knows? I'm just saying it wouldn't be the worst thing to happen that week. Then everyone has to tell fun stories about me, except Alicia because she has too many where I end up looking like a moron. Maybe everyone could read fun limericks instead to avoid any stories that compromise the dignified character that I create later in life.

Also, and this is very important, kids can wear whatever the hell they want. I was in uncomfortable tights, shoes, and velvet dresses from ages 5-11 and I absolutely hated it. Tights are the most uncomfortable thing to wear (as demonstrated in my untimely demise), so no one should have to suffer when attending my wake. Although, it would be hilarious to make all the women dress in hideous velvet dresses, so do that. And what the hell make the men wear tights, so that they know for once the discomfort us women live with during the workday. Lastly, and most important of all my other simple demands, there has to be Maurice

Lenell cookies and free pop, because that's how you know it's a party.

A Field Trip to Bourbon Street

NERD ALERT: WHEN I WAS in the sixth grade I wasn't the coolest person at school. I was what you would call, a nerd. Not so nerdish that I fit the mold of pocket protector/glasses/braces nerd, although that was my dream when I was younger. Cool accessories that you can customize with colorful rubber bands and purchase protective cases for? Sign me up! But I was middle of the pack- got good grades but was socially in-tune with pop culture and societal norms, having just enough exposure for the mean girls to make fun of me mercilessly at their will. (Insert pity party here).

One could argue from looking at my class photo that it was my outward appearance that made me a target. With my old-lady sweater from Kohl's and my chubby face and belly, the only thing that would make this image worse is an above the shoulder haircut with bangs- which I definitely had. There should be a law in the United States banning sixth-grade girls from getting bangs. I don't know why their mothers allow such a travesty. Perhaps it is a desperate attempt to cling to the babyface that is quickly morphing into a hideous beast before their very eyes? Maybe it's a safe way to provide their screaming, growth spurting, hot-tempered little monsters into creating some form of identity. Allowing them to look hideous in their class photo with hair framing their face 1/3 of the way past their hairline is a passive-aggressive way to get back at all the hours of arguing over things like which movie ratings are appropriate for a twelve-year-old girl, and why it isn't ok to stay out until 10 PM with boys on the front stoop. Whatever the case, my bangs did not help my puberty stricken face in the slightest. But it wasn't as if I was alone. There were twenty-two other faces in Immaculate Heart of Mary's 1997 sixth grade class photo, and I can tell you with great confidence that not one of those faces went on to be a model, although some might have gone on to bang some.

I was never quite sure what I did to entice the name calling, whispering behind my back, and shitty looks I'd received, but after years of hating my tormentors and wishing them tragic deaths where they get Bonnie Bell lip gloss poisoning, or stuff their bras with poisonous Kleenex, I've moved on and chalked it up to the wonderfully blessed times of puberty. To this day though, I still contest that sixth-grade girls are by far the meanest creatures on this planet. Some of them cling on to those hormones that cause them to hate, turning them into evil women, but most of them shed their snakeskin to go on to live normal lives as decent ladies.

Throughout life, when I come across a clique of women, I can typically classify them into one of three main categories. Some are still mean little girls trapped in insecure grown-up bodies, using their time at work to make others feel bad because they are unconfident and don't know how to do their job. They usually go to lunch together and talk shit all day, every day. Instead of spending their time figuring out how to do their job, they complain about people who they work with in such a way that it makes them look like a saint for putting up with it. You know the type, and you probably are hiding at your desk right now avoiding that group in the office if you are unfortunate enough to work with them.

Then there are the cliques of women in the workplace who are awesome and remind you of your group of best friends. They are the ones who know how to handle their job, know every person's history and weaknesses in the office, but won't use it unless provoked. If it weren't for the fact that you see these women forty-plus hours a week, you would consider hanging out with them sometime after work. But then again you don't want to mess with the perfect set up you have of your work-friendship, a truly sacred union.

The third group of women is technically not a group, but a classification nonetheless. These are the nerdy types, who keep to themselves but when prodded, reveal that they are very, very smart and good at their jobs. The only problem is that they are so quiet and introverted, that they typically go unnoticed, unless you need help with a project and have to ask for their help, just like when you would sweet-talk the class nerd to give you the answers to last night's geography homework.

Up until this point in my life, I had only witnessed these three types of women. So when it came time to interview with Melanie and Julie, the only two women who made up the Sales Analyst department for ViewIt, a TV show listing website that was part of the almighty

Tribune Company. I was nervous to see which group these ladies would fall into, fearing the mean girl class, but hoping for the awesome group. What I didn't realize though was that there was a fourth group in which my future coworkers fell into, which was supreme working machines with abs- the rarest of the groups.

I snuck underground the day of my interview at ViewIt. I had been working at IHD for almost two years, and I was days away from going crazy with boredom. Each day I would stare out the window at the beautiful, gothic-designed Tribune Tower and imagine all the fun, exciting jobs I could get if I just had a journalism degree. (Sidenote: This was about a year before the industry of journalism sank like the Titanic and *Buzzfeed* took over as everyone's main source of daily news. If you are reading this in the future- journalism is what us old folks used to find out information about current events). I thought that if I could just get a job inside the building, I would magically find the grit and perseverance to work my way into a cool writing job where I could provide comical insight with a daily column. So when my friend and fellow *Redeye Royalty* comrade had a position open up in his company that was located in the tower, I worked my way into an interview.

The day of the interview, I was suspiciously not dressed like a slob, which I feared would tip off my bosses at IHD that I was up to something. I had a skirt on for one, which probably was the first time I had ever worn a skirt at that job aside from my interview. I had a nice blouse on, and my trusty, albeit less new-looking discounted Ann Taylor Loft suit jacket shoved into my work bag, wrapped around my heels.

In order to travel next door to my interview without being noticed, I walked down to lower Michigan Avenue, which you may know as the street they used to film one of the Batman movies. It is drippy and creepy down there, with glaring yellow lights and dumpsters along the edges where the skyscrapers throw out their trash. This is where I prepared for my big get-in-the-tower interview. I quickly changed out of my gym shoes, threw on my suit jacket, fluffed my hair, and walked back above ground but a block past IHD so that I would be unseen by coworkers. Kind of like one of the many rats hiding on lower Michigan Avenue, I was unnoticed but determined.

I got the job and got the hell out of the state job, which I now miss dearly only for its combination of growing vacation hours for every year worked plus rollover vacation days. (One woman who worked there for over twenty years would take the entire month of December off each year because she had so much vacation time. She probably could have taken the entire winter off with the lack of work done at that place, but I guess one month is the appropriate amount of time to take off each year when you work for the state.) I was energized, revitalized, and eager to start a new job where I would be working instead of trying to look busy. Oh, how foolish one can be when their dreams get in the way.

My role as a sales analyst had two main duties: RFPs and ad placements. You see girls and boys, when a website has ad space and is popular enough to get people to advertise on its site, it first sends a team of salespeople out to sell ad space, ensuring the ads are seen a certain amount of times. Then, when a company considers advertising with them, the sales analyst (that's me), sends out requests for proposals, or RFPS, to estimate the cost and amount of times each ad will be viewed. If the company agrees, they then send over their ad images, and the sales analyst works with the operations team to make them swoop in from the side, pop up out of nowhere, and appear at peak hours of web viewing. Simple enough, yes? One would think. To this day I'm not really sure how I did these things with such a low grasp of how they were to get done. It was a hell of a lot of work to put forth into something that could easily be sent away by clicking a little 'x' in the top right corner.

For me, RFPs were like horrible brain puzzles that I did not have the logic skills to succeed. You would have to do a combination of paid ads, free ads, and various ad sizes to get the price to what the client wanted. None of my RFPs balanced out, and I could not grasp the concept no matter how many hours Melanie and Julie spent teaching me. At first, they were kind and patient, and I was not stressed because they were still checking my work before it went out. But slowly the safety net was removed, and my work was consistently splattering on the concrete floor. What stressed me out the most though was that this three-person department handled the workload of what should have been a nine-person staffed team. Because I was not a machine like the other two, things were slipping up, and I was working later and later.

What was most intimidating of all was that Melanie and Julie were a powerhouse of workers. These women would come in at 9, work non-stop until lunch, work out for an hour in the basement gym, eat, and work until 5 PM without pause. I tried catching them in the act of slacking countless times, but every time their asses were seated, they were working. And not my brand of working, where you work on something, get frustrated, and relax for a few hours on Facebook until it's time for lunch. Come to think of it; I don't even recall running into them on the way to the bathroom, which also makes me believe they were machines.

Melanie and Julie could have easily been cruel to me, especially since I wasn't carrying my weight in workload, but the entire year they were patient and polite, though we never bonded. For Christmas, I brought in gifts, not knowing what the protocol was, and none of them exchanged presents, so I kept my gifts hidden in my purse. Had I been more paranoid, I would have feared they had a big cool-kids-only Christmas party sans Connie, but I'm pretty sure they didn't because that would have broken their concentration.

So there I was, the uncool, no-talent hack stress-eating Twizzler Cherry Bites all day long in the tower. My early ambition to climb to the top was at a standstill because my ego was knocked over on account that I had no freaking clue how to do my job well. Someone should have told me straight up, "You don't have it kid." and I would have flown out of that place. But no one did, and my bruised ego decided to flop around like a dying fish until I gave it my all, or at least one year, which was my new standard of time allotted in a crappy job. With all the insecurities flying around in my head about how I was the slow one (both with my actual work and in the spin class I would take with Melanie and Julie), I felt like a pudgy sixth grader all over again.

And then we had a field trip.

Our boss Karen, an older, well-dressed classy woman stationed in New York and whom I only spoke to in our teleconference all staff meetings, declared that we would be heading to New Orleans for a big data conference called CTAM. I have no idea what the conference was for exactly, but I got a coffee mug from it that says *ZuZu's Jazz Club*, so something to do with tech or jazz? The entire ViewIt sales team would be going- the two machines, three salespeople, the boss lady, and me.

Work trips, in general, have all the excitement and liveliness of school field trips. You get to see your classmates in an unexplored arena, classroom rules are thrown out the window, and you can dress differently than your typical blouse and plaid skirt. The popular boy, who always looks cool even though he is typically forced to wear the exact same uniform as every other boy, suddenly is highlighted even more in a halo and angel wings that is a Michael Jordan 23 Bulls jersey and a backwards baseball cap.

Field trips are also the time for those quiet kids to reinvent themselves- all they need is one bold act to set them apart from the herd and move up a class into the cool kid group. Occasionally in school, the field trip gods would smile down upon a lowly classmate and offer them a gift. One time a girl in my first-grade class busted her face open on a rather gruesome ice skating trip, making her set for life in classroom fame. My closest brush with field trip stardom was a trip to the nature preserve in fifth-grade where I slipped in some mud and fell in a pond. That granted me recognition until Christmas break when one girl got a perm and my pond drowning fame was forgotten.

We arrived at New Orleans and were treated to the fanciest things. We stayed at the W Hotel in the French Quarter, where we had our all-staff meeting in a fancy pants conference room that had fancy Tea Forte tea bags. I didn't even drink tea at the time, but I was so impressed with the unique pyramid-shaped packaging that I shoved five in my purse when no one was looking.

We spent the first day in one long meeting, where we each shared a report in a PowerPoint presentation, each topic decreed by Karen. I met each of the salespeople in person, and even though I had already pictured what they looked like during our weekly teleconferences, Melanie and Julie warned me that they would look nothing like I pictured. And they were right (as usual).

The closest image I came to was Monica, the LA sales representative. I hated her voice, attitude and now face. I feel that any person reading this can relate and that I don't really have to go on for you to comprehend that instantaneous decision of hate based on an initial conversation with a person. But since I hope to get paid by the word for this book Charles Dickens style, I shall go on.

The first time I talked to Monica, I had been at my position for exactly three days. Melanie and Julie were on their lunch break finding a cure for cancer while working on their core, so I was alone in the office. Monica calls, mind you this is the first time I ever talk to her, and she replies, "Yeah hi, do you know if the $10K Glee RFP went out yet? They want to add five more, can you do that like now?" to my "Hello! This is Connie." I process that she is someone I am to be working with, and try to piece together what she is talking about from there. After I find an email with the words matching what she is saying, I tell her I can try, which sends her into a tailspin of frenzy. Melanie and Julie's work radar went off at that moment, and they appeared out of nowhere, saving me from the rude lady on the phone.

Had I known how unimportant she was, and that I was going to suck so badly at that job, I would have hung up on her after the Yeah hi. Who says that? "Yeah hi." Assholes, that's who. Yeah hi is basically the condensed form of the sentence, "Yeah hi I'm a douchebag about to be an asshat to you, so sit down and assume the position." Yeah hi. Psssh. You're cool.

Monica looked pretty much how I pictured- thin but now fit, stressed out looking, and wearing lots of overpriced makeup with lots of pricey attachments, none of which are needed to sell advertisements on a small website. She wasn't blonde though, more of a fake redhead. And she was about 75 years old looking even though she was in her forties. (Maybe not 75, but that's what you get for not being nice on the phone!).

Nick was younger than he looked. A guy from New York but not New York City, on the phone he sounded like Gil from the Simpsons- a sad guy trying to make a sale, with a strong reek of desperation. Nick came in trying to reinvent the wheel of online ad sales, and last I heard, it hasn't changed at all. White hair, oddly tanned, and on the thin side, which I couldn't tell if it was from eating right or from surviving on ramen noodles for too long.

Brad was the ringleader of the sales team and was way older than I imagined. On the phone, Brad sounded like a cool guy, late 20s, and always very hyper on Fridays and very tired on Mondays. In person, he was all these things- just in his mid-40s. Brad was from Colorado, which means if you want to base your life on where you will feel the youngest- go to Colorado right now. Brad was tan and fit, in an- 'I've been outside having fun all day with my kids, not from stressing out or running on a treadmill in the office basement' kind of way.

Brad was also a charmer. Everyone would be more willing to write up his RFPs because he would get excited, and pass it on to you. He would also say things like please and thank you. But it was mainly his charm that made him a great salesperson. He was one of those people who make everyone like him, not in a crush/romantic way, but like the popular boy in school. Even if you don't romantically like him, you're super excited if he is assigned to the seat next to you on the bus. One time in Chicago, Brad took Melanie, Julie and I to a concert with some of his clients who were our age. After the concert, he found out where the band was going after, took us there, and proceeded to find a way for us to hang out with the band. And the band was excited to hang out with him. THAT'S how much of a charmer he was.

After an afternoon of meetings where I assessed and judged all of my coworkers, we went out to eat at a four-star restaurant in the French Quarter. The best thing I can say about my time working for ViewIt was that Karen took us to the nicest restaurants. I lived in Chicago all my life, but I went to more deliciously decadent downtown spots in that year than I had my entire existence in the 606.

Eating with the group of coworkers the first night was like a junior high dance. For the first hour, everyone was silent and awkward, even though we co-existed with each other every day. Brad got the conversation going, but it still took a while for the happy hour cocktails to sink in. I was silent and focused on what to order, knowing that if I ever came back to NOLA, I'd be eating at grungy pizza places that were open until three in the morning, not at a place where the waiter knew the history of the building and folded your napkin when you went to the bathroom.

The other reason no one talks the first night when ordering dinner is that everyone is intensely concentrated on what to order. To be clear: no one is thinking about what they want to eat (unless they don't care about losing their job like normal people!) but what will impress the boss without breaking the bank. So much thought goes into ordering in front of coworkers, it's insane.

First you have to worry about the price. You want to match your price to what you conservatively think you are worth to the company. Last person on the totem pole? Order a salad. Big time CEO that just saved the company? You've earned that porterhouse steak. Some people might think they are steak worthy, but one look from your boss will tell you if you've earned that entrée. It is better to undershoot than to go big, but you don't want to convey that you think you are a cheap pasta, because that can make your manager think you aren't pulling your weight.

Next there is the food itself. To make sure I order something office appropriate, I check the five senses. Touch: Do I need my hands for this? As much as I like buffalo wings, it is probably best not to order them. Taste: If you have coworkers who like to try each other's food, don't order something weird that will leave a bad taste in their mouth. The key is to stand out for flavor, not for weird food preferences. Smell: Do NOT order the smelliest fish in the sea, no matter how many breath mints you have with you. Sight: No one wants to watch you slurp a spaghetti strand. It's not cute unless you are a cartoon dog. Sound: Crunchy food makes it hard to hear. Do you really want to miss out on company gossip because you are chomping at a fiber-rich salad? No. Sound: SLLLUUUURRRP. That's the sound of you eating soup, which leads to you getting fired, which will lead you to a soup kitchen, where you can slurp all the soup you want.

Last there are points for originality. Similar to price where you don't want to go insane, you want to land somewhere right on the axis of interesting, but not overly absurd. I chose the scallops in a fancy sauce with a side of schmancy potatoes. Sounds boring, but given my affinity for being a crappy worker and that most likely I would never return to NOLA proper, I didn't want to chance it with a strange entrée that may have tasted bad. There were a lot of mistakes I made at ViewIt, but ordering those delicious scallops is what probably kept me from getting fired, despite a rather poor review at the end of the year.

As it turns out, the ViewIt team was big on sharing each other's' food, and mine was by far the best pick. Monica had an expensive steak that was overdone. Honestly, who orders steak in a sea-bordering state?

Morons, that's who. Brad, Melanie, and Julie each had a carefully selected, non-smelling fish entrée, and Karen ordered an expensive fish special, modified to her taste. As the plates went around, everyone marveled at the scallop potato masterpiece that was on my plate. And then my plate passed to Karen, and everyone waited with bated breath to see her decree, which was manifested in the form of a raised eyebrow, indicating surprise and approval. To this day, I remember that eyebrow raise. I couldn't tell you whether my own mother looked proud at my college graduation, or if she was there, but I know that Karen enjoyed my scallops. (Sidenote: relax, mom, you were totally at my graduation, I know. I'm using this sentence for dramatic effect!)

Once the cool kids at the table deemed that I was ok, the night improved. Everyone started talking to me, drinks came, and we shared some of the most delicious desserts in the world. As we exited the restaurant, Brad, the self-declared cruise captain came up to me and said to hang back. It was like the cool kid himself said I could sit in the back of the bus with the other cool kids. I was so in. The older/boring people headed back to the hotel, while Brad, Melanie, Julie, Nick and I headed to find something to do in New Orleans at night. Brad explained to me that he usually puts himself in charge of something fun to do for the group and will keep you out late, but will personally give you a wakeup call the next morning, so you don't sleep in and look like an idiot. I assured him I'd be fine, and we headed to the conference's big event at House of Blues.

The only time I have been to the House of Blues before was in Chicago when I went to see Lucky Boys Confusion, a fantastic band of my high school days, similar to Fallout Boy, but even more awesome. The scene at House of Blues New Orleans CTAM event had a much different crowd, but dare I say was much wilder than a rock concert filled with hormone-crazed teens. To this day I do not underestimate the power of booze plus New Orleans music plus hundreds of IT staff from around the world released out of their cubicles for a wild and crazy time. More people were making out at the CTAM event than I remember seeing at the Lucky Boys concert, and I'm pretty sure some people may have even passed first base. Within five minutes of entering, Brad came up to us at the bar with a strand of drink tickets so long it looked like he won big at the *Chuck-E-Cheese* Skee Ball game.

The same rules for eating with coworkers applies to ordering drinks, but since I have *McDonald's* taste buds in a scallops and fancy potatoes world, I always panic and order vodka cranberry when I am with mixed company. That is the most boring drink you could ever get in New Orleans, but I was trying to play it safe considering I had a lanyard with my name-tag hanging around my neck.

We sailed through the Skee Ball tickets in about an hour. Nick was the most noticeably drunk, while Melanie and Julie seemed un-phased, despite having the waistlines of small children, they were unsurprisingly successful at holding their liquor as they were at everything else in life.

Brad escorted our group out of the tourist bar and down a dark alley, to a heavy metal bar, *Ye Olde Original Dungeon*. He found this bar by asking some locals where to go, which led us down an alley and over a bridge across a small pond/swamp and into a dark, seedy looking dive bar. As you enter, there was a giant cage, the kind you use to capture people and hold them in your basement. At first glance, we were all frightened. But after a few of the house special O-Bombs, an early 2000s classic shot of Bacardi O and Red Bull, (the drink of future cardiovascular patients) I realized that the heavy metal music and the naked mannequins wrapped in bondage were merely a theme. Just like in Epcot where they have a different bar for every country, the dungeon was just a bar with a theme of creepy. In actuality, I was probably safer having beers and talking to a bartender with tattoo sleeves and giant ear plugs than I would be at a tourist bar on Bourbon street, with scads of drunken assholes and the potential of getting roofied or puked on. I would have been pleased spending the rest of the night in the scary bar, but Brad decided it was time to eat and check out what was happening on Bourbon street. At this time two things were clear to me: 1. Dungeon bars are fun. 2. I was drunk.

I've examined the following events that unfolded on varying degrees of soberness and to the best of my knowledge, this was my thought process in what is now known simply as the New Orleans trip by my friend Anna who laughs uncontrollably whenever this story is mentioned.

So we stumble out of the alley and into the crowds of Bourbon street. I am immediately thrown off of my senses and flashback to my college days, drunkenly stumbling around Wrigleyville among crowds of drunks trying to hook up with each other. This sends me into a spout of boredom similar to the ones I would have when my single girlfriends were busy trying to find a hot guy at the bar. I'd often find ways to entertain myself by finding random/non-threatening strangers to talk to, or steal bar signs and try and hide them in my coat, or by writing "boys suck" on the bathroom wall when my boyfriend in college wouldn't pick up the phone to his slurring girlfriend at 2 o'clock in the morning. This extroverted, more boisterous version of me was once categorized as 'Bonnie' the drunken, more ridiculous version of myself.

By the time we get to the shitty tourist bar, I'm slightly pissed. Brad, who I realize, has provided a fun and enjoyable evening, living up to his word. However, I am irritated that my only request, to drink a Hurricane, THE signature drink of New Orleans, was refuted by Brad and deemed too touristy. "Who made you the boss of my life? Newsflash Brad, we are in a tourist city, and if I want to drink a Hurricane and set it on top of a postcard while I wear a fanny pack, then I'll do as I please." These are the things I would have said, had I not been too busy trying not to notice how wobbly the floor was.

Angry and bored, I was determined to make sure the scallops I ordered seven hours earlier were not in vain. We entered a bar where a live band was playing Black Eyed Peas, which if I'm not mistaken, have no connection to New Orleans whatsoever. The group, which dwindled down to Melanie, Brad and Nick (Julie was smart enough to leave at a respectable time, she's probably a CEO of something by now) entered and headed straight for the bar. I was the last one in line, but somewhere from the front door to the bar I, or rather, Bonnie, was pulled by a force stronger than myself. The band had shifted from its traditional cultural songs of Fergie to an even more familiar song- "Sexy Back." The force of the song was stronger than if I had drank

100 Hurricanes, and I was led to the stage by a need to dance. I crawled up the dark wooden stairs and staggered right up to the singer who was in the middle of belting out "Take it to the chorus!" He looked surprised to see me almost as if he didn't have a note on his setlist saying some drunk girl would come up on stage and try to dance with him. But like a true performer worthy of singing Justin Timberlake, he grabbed me by the waist, and I danced up on him while he continued on with the song.

Meanwhile in the crowd, cruise director Brad was looking concerned that he lost one of his party crew members. As I looked out in between ass shakes and fist pumps, I proceeded to see Brad and Melanie, jaws to the floor, watching in what I will assume to be utter awe that I chose to grace the good people of New Orleans with my dancing abilities. It was as if I ordered five plates of scallops and potatoes on stage and passed them around; they were that impressed.

When the song was over, my dance partner booted me off the stage, undoubtedly because I was too good of a dancer for him to keep up. I was lauded as the coolest coworker in the world and went to sleep a victor of the field trip. Brad, true to his word, woke me up just in time for me to run a brush through my hair and brush my teeth, which didn't help me from smelling like I died. At breakfast the whole group was a buzz about the night before, and Karen was surprisingly pleased to hear I had danced on stage, which makes me think that her previous work feedback of 'be more vocal' and 'take action in your work' could have been easier to follow if she had just said, 'Get wasted and shake your ass.' Regardless, I had won the field trip and was now recognized as one of the fun coworkers, making a name for myself that lasted a whole 12 hours until the next night when Nick got hammered and did the worm in the middle of Bourbon street. That's the trouble with popularity; it can be very fleeting.

Beware the Leather Jacket

Fashion is about dressing according to what's fashionable. Style is more about being yourself.

-Oscar de la Renta

This looks clean!

-Connie O'Reyes

DRESS FOR THE JOB you want, not the job you have. This is a famous quote thrown around in job interview workshops which implies that in order to become successful one must look successful. A fake it 'til you make it approach for the workplace if you will. If there's one thing twelve years in private school wearing plaid skirts and polo shirts has taught me, it's that I don't know how to dress well. What I possess in other talents I lack in the ability to put outfits together that give off any message other than saying, "I'm dressed."

I've struggled with this for years and tend to lean toward the 'form follows function' mentality in my wardrobe selections. After high school, I donned the classic hoodie and jeans ensemble when I was in class. Weekends were all about showing off cleavage, which up until recently I thought was the only fashion accessory needed. Did you know there is more ways to change your look from day to evening that doesn't simply involve unbuttoning your shirt at the top? Neither did I!

Now that I'm technically a grown-up, I am getting more and more pressure to develop a 'style' that suits me. For some reason, I feel that this is a necessary part of being an adult- being able to look at your wardrobe and pull out an outfit that is professional looking for work, yet also includes your personal charm. The New York and Company blouses and Target Mossimo black ankle pants I have don't really say anything. They are kind of mute and dull.

The problem with fashion and working in an office is the intersection of comfort. Sitting in a desk chair all day in fluorescent lighting is the pits. There is no comfort to be found in an office setting. You are either at your desk in front of your computer, occasionally spilling coffee on your poorly accessorized outfit, or you're in a meeting sitting up straight so that you don't accidentally slump down and fall asleep while your boss is talking. Then, you go home and most likely have to walk to public transportation. Lord help me if I have to walk more than .13 miles in heels. My toes shoot out pain, and I hobble down the street like a zombie because my feet are too fat to find comfortable heels. (Sidenote: Can we all agree that women who say high heels are comfortable on them because they have high arches are liars? I don't care if your foot is shaped like Barbie's, you cannot tell me that wearing a pair of Jimmy-Manolo-Tino's are comfier than a pair of gym shoes. These women are lying. If I ever had to investigate a company for embezzlement, I'd look at everyone's shoes and whoever had the most uncomfortable shoes on, men or women, I would ask if they felt comfortable and if they said yes I would peg them for fraud. NO ONE likes wearing uncomfortable shoes. No one.)

I'm not a total dweeb when it comes to fashion. I know where the Macy's dress section is on State Street, and I have a couple of cute scarves that I pull out for style instead of necessity. One time I bought this really cute and cool leather jacket that made me look super hip. I wore it all the time- work, parties, dinners, everywhere. It was my 'I'm so cool now that I have a leather jacket' jacket. But then I started noticing my confidence level was having some issues- the issue being it was too freaking high. I turned into a bully and started terrorizing people. Once at a party, I knocked the top of my brother-in-law's beer bottle with the bottom of mine so it would explode everywhere and he would have to chug it. The problem though was that we were in a crowded bar and he wasn't paying attention, so he just looked at it sadly while I laughed my head off. Another time, I got into it with a coworker.

To be fair, this dude had it coming. His name was Brandon and he was a pain in the butt. You know the person in the office when you go into the break room and get coffee you hope they're not there but they always are in there when you go in and they're always telling some outrageous story you think is a lie and also not funny? That was Brandon. Puke.

The office was planning a retirement party for the department head and our team was assigned to put it together. This involved a lot of mindless crap like calling a caterer, picking out chicken or beef sandwiches, and counting how many pieces of cake would be needed. You know, strenuous brain exercises like that. Brandon, the office receptionist, was in charge of these things and knew the party was happening, yet took off for vacation the week everything had to be planned, leaving me to decide between chocolate or vanilla ice cream. Fine. No Problem. Except, when he returned, crybaby diva was upset because I went with a different caterer than the gross food he always picks. For days I heard comments like, "Well Papa Pasta always gives us extra utensils." And "Papa Pasta has the best macaroni salad (they don't. It's mayonnaise with some noodles.) He drove me crazy, especially since I was the one helping this fool out when he took off the one week where he was actually needed and couldn't be replaced by a voicemail account. So after like two days of this, he comes to my desk asking for the food order receipt and starts to complain that the Papa Pasta receipts are made from unicorn hair or something and I flip. Now, normal Connie would have sat in anger, G-chatted a friend and gone into a five adjective long curse storm about what type of asshole this guy was. But my leather jacket was hanging off my chair, oozing confidence and power into my brain. So I SLAMMED my hand on my desk, looked the jerk dead in his eyes and said loudly "You know what? If YOU wanted to order from Papa Pasta, YOU should have ordered it then!" And hand to God, I thought I made the poor guy cry. He looked at me in shock, shut his trap, and walked out the door. Now, fine, whatever, this guy may have had hard times in his life and needed an outlet to vent his life frustrations, fine, I get that. I also get that when someone does something nice for you, you don't reciprocate by being a douchebag. Regardless, I yelled at a coworker, something I've never dared to do, and probably shouldn't have. I knew that the jacket had to go, and I gave it to my sister to wear and wreak havoc on the world. Her name is Kim Jong-un and she works somewhere in North Korea.

It's not that I don't *want* to be stylish, it's just that I haven't learned how to put it all together, no matter how many episodes of What Not to Wear I've seen in my life.

Although I may never become the 'fashionable one' in the office, I have compiled a few basic, and I stress basic, rules for myself to follow as I approach the age of where it is no longer cute to wear pajama pants in public. (Thank you God for yoga pants!).

1. Never go to the office with wet hair, even if you think it will dry by the time you get to work.

2. Never have dirty hair in the office. That is what dry hair shampoo is for.

3. Don't wear t-shirts, hoodies, or flip flops to the office. Just don't.

Lately, I have been dressing with clothes that look like I am pregnant with child, even though the only thing in my gut is leftover pizza. I've put on a few pounds that I am working on shedding, but until that happens, my rule is that I will stop buying clothes that make me look like I am trying to hide my gut, like flowy tops, and instead buy better garments that will make me look stylish and well structured. Like my fashion icon, Mindy Kaling.

Mindy Kaling is, how do I put this? Mindy Kaling is the coolest person ever. Not only does she do a million projects and defied Hollywood's norms, she also has clothes that are on fleek. (Note: when this book is read years later, fleek will be outdated, so feel free to insert a new phrase. I hope it's better than previous versions of this phrase including 'the shit' and 'bomb ass.' Those were weak as hell). She's not afraid to do something exotic, like mix bold colors with crazy patterns, yet every outfit worn by her is tied back to her personal style. Yes she is a celebrity and probably has brilliant stylists that do all this for her, but I'm pretty sure she gets to have the final say, which is always an amazing statement. Swoon.

Because I am not a celebrity (outside of my head at least), I dismiss my shortcomings by way of normalcy, but that is not true. I've worked with some colleagues who look like they are going to fashion week in New York City, even though they are just sitting in a monthly meeting about marketing budgets. On the same floor that I work at, there is this guy who dresses like he is going to a modeling shoot after work. It's outstanding. I constantly find myself wishing that he were a lady so that I could ask him for women's fashion advice on where to shop.

Someday, it will all magically click and I will understand how to dress myself as well as the celebrities. Until then I will continue to try and pass off my Gap V-neck long sleeve shirts as business casual.

Carrie Bradshaw is a Liar

WHEN I WAS TWELVE, I loved to read because I enjoyed praise from adults and liked looking smart. You were probably expecting a more refined explanation of why an author got into reading, but that's my reason. I liked how adults would marvel at my advanced reading level. The school librarian, Mrs. Payne, would let me eat lunch in the library in exchange for helping her put returned books back on the shelves. It was a deal that was beneficial for me because lunchtime in middle school is like Alcatraz in its heyday- mass mayhem and a slim chance of survival. In the library, there was a reading comprehension program disk that was taken on the first version of a Mac that ever existed. Every book in the library had a 10 question comprehension test that quizzed you on your knowledge of a book. The threshold to pass was something ridiculously small, like 50%, but I was determined to ace every book test that I could take. This was before the concept of cheating corrupted my innocent mind, and I had not yet discovered the wonders of Cliff Notes, so I would go about things the honest route- by reading a book and taking the quiz.

At first I started out within the range of my comprehension- Secret Garden, Little Women, but then I started hitting the hard stuff. My selection process was scanning the large sized books as I was shelving, and picking out the stuffiest, most adult looking books, which included some loser named Leo Tolstoy. Stupid Tolstoy was the only test I failed- I got 4 out of 10 on the quiz about Anna Karenina, which, if you've ever read Tolstoy or any Russian literature, you may understand that it's incomprehensible. Nonetheless, I conceded to my low score years later when someone mentioned the ending in which Anna Karenina dies (spoiler alert- she dies.) to which I responded, "She died?!!"

I was on a reader's high for quite a while there until one summer trip, when my Uncle John ruined Henry David Thoreau's *Walden* for me.

Uncle John was a Catholic priest. A loveable, kind soul, he had my mom's eyes, giant Irish hands and a smoker's cough. (Sad spoiler alert- he passed away when I was in college. Everyone on my mom's side has passed away for the most part. It's because they're Irish. If they didn't, whose funeral would we go to on the weekends?) My mom would plan family vacations with him, which was great because he had a chance to bond with his favorite niece (me, and possibly my sister if I was napping.) Plus there would be an extra person in the car to drive my dad, the minivan driver, insane during our long drives outside of Illinois.

During the summer of my family's trip to the Poconos, (a very nature filled place in Pennsylvania, which did not have the best TV reception as I recall) I was carrying around *Walden* all over the place with me in hopes that my Uncle John would see it and give me the praise one should give a puberty-stricken girl who decided to read Henry David Thoreau over the summer instead of doing something more entertaining like getting into drugs or alcohol. This praise would be especially noteworthy since Uncle John was not one to give praise as generously as my parents, who have been giving me words of encouragement ever since I learned to use the potty.

I was sitting in the living room of the vacation home rental, reading in the dim light of the closed patio door that was shielding me from the nature I was reading about. Uncle John wandered over from his room and set me up for my long anticipated recognition.

"Whatcha reading?" He asked as he stood over me from behind the couch, blocking the little light I had.

"*Walden.*" I said as nonchalantly as I could.

"Yeeach. Thoreau! Never got into him. Too bland."

Now mind you, this came from a man whose job it was to read aloud at least one Old Testament passage every day. As he walked away to eat all of the snacks my mom had packed for the entire vacation, I realized that I too thought Thoreau was a tad dull. More importantly, even if I had suffered through his literature, my uncle wouldn't think me better for it, and would still knock off Thoreau as a boring guy stuck in the woods. So it got in my head that Thoreau was boring, and to this day I have not had the desire to pick up *Walden* ever again.

Extensive research on *Walden*, which I have done by skimming the first paragraph on this subject in Wikipedia, says the following: *"**Walden** (first published as **Walden; or, Life in the Woods**), by noted transcendentalist Henry David Thoreau, is a reflection upon simple living in natural surroundings. The work is part personal declaration of independence, social experiment, voyage of spiritual discovery, satire, and manual for self-reliance."* This is exactly the guidance I needed when living in Bloomington, Illinois, where I failed as a freelance writer.

One with Nature

Despite eating at a bunch of fancy places on *ViewIt's* dime, I realized I wasn't having any fun as a sales analyst. At the same time, my soon-to-be husband had recently moved to Bloomington, Illinois for a new job, so I figured now was as good of a time as any to become a freelance writer and spit out a couple famous essays and novels. Carrie Bradshaw made it look as effortless as running in six-inch stiletto heels, so why couldn't I? Chompers and I packed our bags and headed down to the center of Illinois.

Bloomington-Normal was one of those double cities that pairs up to offer all the amenities of a small suburb. Home to the Illinois State University Redbirds, it has about 130,000 humans in it, which is also the number of people in line at any given Starbucks in downtown Chicago. To most, it was a nice small city where you could start a family and buy a house at an affordable price. To me, it was a cabin in the woods where people needed to trap their food and beat their dirty clothes out on river rocks.

Now, I'm about to spit some mad Chicago love with a dose of stuck up city folk talk, so just picture me with a Bulls cap on my head, blue and orange Chicago Bears face paint, a pair of the thick framed sunglasses the Blues Brothers wore, and a city flag tattoo down my forearm, which is how I have been dressed this entire time.

Andrew had lived in Bloomington for almost a year before I moved there, but since all of his family, friends, and social life were in Chicago, he would always come up to see me instead of the reversed. I often asked if he had some Bloomington side chick he was hiding, but he contested by questioning my sanity, followed by the simple explanation that I wouldn't like the conditions in which he lived. I didn't believe him until the first night in our brand new apartment, where we both had to sleep on his former bed- an old futon mattress with bars sticking in our back. The next day movers unpacked my queen-sized bed while I sketched out plans to decorate our new place into a home worthy of the Pritzkers.

As soon as the necessities were unpacked and situated, I ventured out in my six oxen wagon in search of sustenance. One of the only things about Bloomington I enjoyed was that every middle-class store in the world was conveniently located on Veterans Parkway, a large street that stretched out from my house to Interstate 55 that would take me to Chicago. I could hit up Target for my everyday needs, browse Pier 1 for crap for the home that I would never actually buy but still enjoyed looking at, purchase a new iPod at Best Buy which I would use never because I gave up running, then finish up the day grocery shopping at Schnuck's, a store that didn't exist in Chicago but was priced the same as the Jewel next to it. All this within a one-mile stretch of street. I was feeling more and more comfortable with each familiar retailer I entered. Yes I was in a city that could fit in my city's pocket, but the Target layout was still the same- ladies' clothes right in front, all the other crap towards the back. If you are ever homesick, I suggest walking through a Target. It will make you feel as if you are on your home turf. Within a month, I was feeling more in place, that is, until I went to Macy's and lost my shit.

Having moved in June and with our wedding coming up in October, I was itching to do our wedding registry. We planned to register at Target and Macy's, and with Andrew being at work all day I headed out to get an idea of what to zap with the registry scanner, otherwise known as the greatest toy in the world. I entered the Macy's on Veterans which was attached to the Eastland Mall and browsed around. The main floor was sectioned off in women's attire- juniors near the mall entrance, older women near the parking lot entrance, and jewelry and bags in the center of the floor for all to enjoy. I circled the purse section before I decided to head up to home goods to see all the pretty dishes and bath towels that would soon be mine. I looked around to locate the escalator, typically found in the center of the store, but to no avail. "That's odd." I pondered and proceeded to circle the outer walls in search of an elevator.

I was halfway around the store before I realized there was no second floor, which I failed to notice when

I ran in from the parking lot. I panicked. I was in a one floor Macy's store. ONE FLOOR. The Macy's on State Street in Chicago has nine floors if you count the lower level, which you do. Where was the home goods section? Where was the fine china? Where was the Frango mints stand?? This log cabin had exactly one floor for men, women, and purses, all lumped together like the lost and found box in the back of a church.

I was a pioneer. This city was an uninhabited territory, and I was there to slash away shrubs and build hospitals out of sticks. I bet somewhere in *Walden*, Thoreau explains how to coexist with an environment that only has a one-floor Macy's. From then on, we traveled back to Chicago pretty much every weekend when I could find an excuse to drive the two-hour trek back to civilization.

I lost the manual for self-reliance

It turns out I was as good as being self-employed as I was running in heels. Having just coasted off the success of Marathon Missfit, I was excited to watch my writing career take off with great ease. I pictured myself drinking delicious coffee, while inquisitively staring out a window, searching for a brilliant sentence to pour out onto my keyboard before getting paid millions of dollars. After a morning bout of writing amazingly crafted sentences, I would stroll about the neighborhood with Chompers, exploring the little city we called home. Then I would have lunch in a cute sandwich shop, writing more words in the afternoon, and cozily greeting my new husband when he came home from work, where he would take me out for happy hour, and we would dine at a nice restaurant around the corner.

Instead, this is how my day looked:

<u>My Busy Schedule of Nothing:</u>

8 AM: half wake up to listen to husband get ready for his work day.

9 AM: Husband leaves. Tell the dog to go to sleep because it's not time to get up yet (Chompers complies).

9:50 AM: Get up, put on the bare minimum of clothes needed to go outside and let the dog out. Feed dog, pour Count Chocula cereal for self, turn on TV.

10 AM: Watch Reba reruns. Promise to write as soon as Reba gets out of her predicament.

11 AM: Find *Roseanne*/Sex in the City/*Will & Grace* rerun to watch. Laptop is still off.

12 PM: Run and throw cereal bowl in sink. Greet husband who came home for lunch.

1 PM: Whole lot of nothin'.

6 PM: Shower!

6:30 PM: Eat dinner with husband and dog. Watch TV.

8 PM: Open up laptop, sit on Facebook and Twitter. Think about, yet do not open Microsoft Word for writing.

10 PM: Watch *Friends* for 3 hours.

1 AM: Go to sleep, exhausted and promising to write the great American novel the next day.

Pathetic. I know.

This path to nowhere led me to eventually skip *Sex and the City* reruns whenever I came across them, and made me hate Carrie Bradshaw to this day. Screw you Carrie! You write a column in a paper, not even on the internet, and you get offered a book deal? You probably didn't even use social media or build up a community around your work! And get out of here with your apartment. There is no way you could afford a place in a gorgeous brownstone walk-up that size in BLOOMINGTON, let alone New York City on some stupid column. I highly doubt your freelance career could pay for one of your Manalo's, let alone an apartment. Rent controlled my ass; you were probably stealing money out of Mr. Big's wallet every chance you got. That's why he moved to Paris! That's why he married Natasha! And another thing. If you were a writer sitting around in New York City, you would be fatter. Smoke all you want stick figure, sitting around all day in your apartment as a writer, you'd be stuffing your face with old cheese found in the fridge. I've been to New York City! I know they have cupcakes there! And you know what? If you were 'suuuuch' a good friend and a fashionista, why did you let Miranda walk around in those hideous suits for men in the first three seasons? HUH? WHY?

This is what watching TV for a year will do to a person.

Voyage of Spiritual Discovery (Through a Near Death Experience)

Bloomington is also where I almost died, and not in the hyperbolic sense. I was driving solo one Sunday night in May back from one of the many necessary trips home to Chicago, and by 'necessary' I mean someone had a BBQ, or my parents were ordering pizza that weekend. Two-thirds of the way back, it started to rain. For some reason, the year we lived in Bloomington was the rainiest spring and summer I have ever seen. On one trip back, Andrew, Chompers and I were halfway from Chicago to Bloomington when a crazy monster storm appeared out of nowhere. It was so bad that everyone on the highway just stopped and pulled over. On a highway. Poor Chompers is still traumatized from that one and sits on our laps whenever there is a downpour.

The day I almost died had a similar storm, only it was harder to tell how bad it was because it was nighttime, and the rain was so heavy I could barely see all the lightning zapping the cornfields surrounding me. Luckily there was no one on the highway, which was unusual because normally on a Sunday evening crazy people are zooming 100mph down I-55, which is well known for its drug trafficking. Call me crazy, but if I were transporting tons of drugs down the highway, I'd be a bit more adhering to the rules of the road, but that's me.

So I was driving along, probably listening to Ke$ha, when all of a sudden the windshield wipers decided they didn't want to do their one job anymore, and just stopped completely. This had never happened before and had I known any better that I purchased the hipster version of windshield wipers that would be lazy and quit without notice; I would not have been driving at night in a monsoon.

Being the professional driver that I am, I did what anyone would do in that situation- I screamed my head off. I was already driving well under the 60mph speed limit, but I slowed it down to a cool 15mph while I continued to scream at the top of my lungs. After a minute of screeching, I went through my options. I could pull over of course, but it was raining so hard I couldn't see the shoulder. I was afraid that if I was near a deep ditch and would go rolling down a hill, like the time in college when I went down a ravine in a golf cart, tumbling twice and losing a flip-flop. Somehow I thought this would be worse. I thought about just stopping where I was, but my fear of someone plowing into my little Toyota Rav4 at 100mph kept my foot on the gas pedal.

I flipped my hazards on and tried putting down the window and sticking my head out. That was just a useful as sticking my head in my shirt, so I rolled up the window and continued to squint through the continuous stream of rainwater washing over my windshield. I should mention that right before the big city lights of Bloomington on the highway there are mainly fields, none of which have street lights, so the only thing I could see other than rain were the road lane markers immediately in front of me when my headlight brights exposed them from the storm.

Sometimes when people are faced with great danger, they turn to Jesus in their time of need. Often in movies you see people in plane turbulence saying a prayer with their seatmate, or sing a powerful hymn as they face a troublesome situation. That's what I did when driving on the I-55 in a storm at night with no working windshield wipers- I talked to Jesus. But not in the way I would have imagined. I started to yell/nag at God's Son, in a repetitive, harsh tone. Almost as if He didn't do the dishes after I had already asked him three times. It was something like, "Jesus? Jesus. Jesus? JESUS. Je-sus. Jesus? Jesus Jesus Jesus Jesus

Jesuuuuuuuss!" And so on. It was odd, and I can safely assume that once I meet my maker, Jesus is going to review certain play by plays of my life with me, starting with this one and ask, "What the hell was that about?" Whatever. It was yet another great life moment completely misconstrued by the glitz and glamor of Hollywood.

What seemed like an eternity later, I spotted a set of rear car lights ahead of me and followed it at a safe distance. I didn't know whether this was a drug dealer coked out and driving with their eyes closed, but I figured if they at least had working windshield wipers they were in better shape than I was. So I followed the red lights for maybe a mile before I came to an off-ramp. I took it and was greeted by a street light that gave me enough visual aid to get to the gas station over the bridge. I parked next to a gas station pump, sat for a good five minutes readjusting my eyesight that had performed perfectly at navigating through buckets of water.

Luckily, the gas station joined with a *McDonald's*. Apparently, in times after a trauma, people do weird things. I ordered a ten piece chicken McNugget meal, with a real Coke, not diet. I figured if I cheated death I was going to go on enjoying life, which for me meant getting a regular Coke and a ton of chicken nuggets. The teenage girl working the counter had no idea I had almost died, but was very kind to me despite my frazzled look and shaking. I was so rattled I think I tried to tip her. She was probably used to weird behavior though and most likely assumed I was a drug trafficker coming off a high.

I sat in the booth, shaking and slowly eating my nuggets when I decided I should call Andrew to get me. Although he was concerned, no matter how riled up a person gets when you tell them that you almost died, it is never enough of what you would prefer. He didn't even thank Jesus! Instead, he asked where I was, which I had to ask the register girl, who explained that I was in Lexington, Illinois.

Andrew said something to the effect of, he'll get me when he feels like it, or at least that's how I interpreted it. In the meantime, I decided I would write off Bloomington and driving on the highway forever and instead start a nice life in Lexington. I would work at the *McDonald's*, and live in a house with several street lights surrounding it in case there ever was another biblical flood; I could easily find it when I walked home, because I would never get in a car again.

I ventured into the adjoining gas station, where the attendants also did not share in the joy of me being alive, so much that I almost turned around to go sit back in the *McDonald's* booth. But I decided that I needed a souvenir to commemorate what would forever be known as THE DAY I ALMOST DIED and found a delightful navy hoodie with a route 66 sign on the front, and a map of the US on the back. I bought the hoodie, decided that my road story was worthy of telling in the trucking section of eateries along the historic highway, and instead of giving up driving, decided I would become a trucker, wearing my hoodie from THE NIGHT I ALMOST DIED as a good luck charm.

I explained this all to Andrew in a shrieking, panicked, shouty voice on the ride home and he was unamused. I calmed down enough until the next morning when we returned to retrieve my death mobile, and I saw that there was a graveyard next door to the *McDonald's*/gas station. Completely creeped out, I decided Lexington was not the town for me after all.

We left Bloomington that year when a plot twist that happens in the next chapter took place. Looking back, I didn't really give Bloomington a good chance to let me fall in love with it. We drove back to Chicago practically every weekend, and every time I had a shot at poking fun at the Podunk town, I took it. In actuality, Bloomington wasn't so bad, and if I really committed, I could have made it awesome. But it was my Walden. I had put the idea of it sucking into my head before I got past the first chapter, and just like how Uncle John ruined a classic for me, I pre-judged a chapter in my life and cast it aside before I gave it a chance. To cheer me up, one might say, "But to be fair Connie, the Macy's only have one level." To which I say, thank you, Jesus, for making me a Chicagoan.

The Ann Taylor Loft Suit Strikes Again

Once upon a time, there was a beautiful princess with a face that was more radiant than the sun, and a brain that would not quit. This lovely maiden traveled her village in search of a job that would fit her like a glass slipper and would allow her to sleep like a beauty during the weekends Armed with a college degree in Marketing and clothed in an Ann Taylor Loft suit; the princess set out to find her one true dream job.

I had just finished my 10 AM morning routine of TV watching and breakfast of honey nut Cheerios when I started to check my email. It was summertime in Bloomington, and the apartment building we lived in was in shambles because the owner had left town due to defaulting on his mortgage and the bank was taking over. No one explained this to us, but we figured out that they were doing construction on the building when a crane pulled in and we heard noises outside louder than the furnace. But since finding an apartment that allows large dogs is such a pain, not to mention moving sucks all together, we waited it out and agreed not to pack up until a wrecking ball came through our front room window, which it almost did.

Every day I would check my email accounts, starting with Gmail and then Hotmail. Even though I only kept my Hotmail account for coupons and to send billing receipts, I still checked it quite often out of sheer boredom and habit. This is why on any given time in the day my Facebook status light is usually green. I hate missing out on mundane things like my old friends' from high schools' seventh baby picture of the day, or my mother-in-law posting memes in Italian, which although I cannot understand, are a nice constant in my day. Hotmail had about 300 unread messages, most of which were expired coupons, but with one new message titled 'Hi from DePaul.'

It was my fairy godmother Joy, my manager from DePaul when I was a student worker battling the smelly fridge. We kept in touch occasionally over the past five years, and as soon as I saw her name, I was immediately excited because I had a feeling something good was about to happen. It was the same feeling I had when I first met Andrew, finished the marathon, and hopefully will have once this book is done. Although her email was short and simple, I sensed the undertone of the message, even though I'm usually terrible at that sort of thing.

But this time was different; this two sentence email was riddled with opportunity, one that I was eagerly waiting for to present itself to me as I sat on my couch next to my bowl of now warm cereal milk. Yes, her email simply stated a conversation came up about past student workers, and she was wondering how I was doing. And yet, in my head I read the following:

Hi Connie! It's your work fairy godmother coming to grant your wish. An opportunity has come up here to work as an analyst and you would be perfect for the role. We are nice here and won't make you work 1,200 hours a week. Tell me you're interested so I can let you know about the job and how you can apply. Also, good job by the way on not making your wish about going to a ball. Those things are the worst- crowded, way over on the girl to guy ratio, and the only dude there thinks he's some sort of prince charming.

How I got this from hey how's it going is beyond me. I wish I was that with it and intuitive all the time, but apparently I only get fleeting flashes of that in my life followed by dozens of awkward moments where I say something moronic, like the time I told my coworker I liked how her hair is growing out and made it sound like I hated her original haircut, to which I back-tracked horribly and made it worse with every sentence I added. "I mean your hair is nice now! But it was also nice when you got it cut! Hair is so nice! You-hair-good! Me go now hide!" UGHHHHH. I still want to hide when I think about that.

Yet I summed up all of my coolness that I would ever have in my life to write her an email that when I re-read it back to myself, did not make me cringe in the slightest. Ok, maybe I should not have added a smiley face. Those are very controversial to use in a networking email, and even if you are very comfortable with your coworkers you still should avoid it, especially if you are a young woman trying to appear professional. However, every rule I've ever read about how to act in the workplace can be argued against, so what the hell do I know? Use all the smiley faces you want. By the time I'm 40, people will only be speaking in fat cat gifs anyway, so you're probably good.

Joy emailed me right back explaining that they had some shifts in recent years and were looking for a new marketing analyst that would work directly with her. By mid-July I was called in for an interview, keeping up with Joy all summer and getting updates from her end as well. This brings me to my first piece of advice to any job seekers, in case anyone accidentally picked up this book thinking they would learn how to get a job.

Network.

It's the buzziest buzzword there is in business. Network to most people means kissing ass and making small talk to strangers to land a job. Yes, that's it exactly, except it doesn't have to sound as slimy as all that. Networking can be as simple as emailing a former boss to let them know you graduated college or texting your friend whose brother works at Apple to see if you could shadow him for the day. Like dating, or how I understand dating to work, you can put in a lot of work and end up getting nowhere with a connection. Sometimes people aren't nice and only network to get help, not give it. Those people are opportunistic asshats and can be spotted as easily as the douche bag in the bar who is trying to take your friend home for a one night stand. In both cases their tongues are where they shouldn't be and they're looking over their shoulder constantly for someone better to come along. But just like knowing which person to sit next to in a city bus, networking takes a little bit of faith and lots of people reading. Find nice people that don't mind helping you, and think of a way to make it worth their time. Networking can feel like a lot of work for nothing, but in the end, might be worth it. Coincidentally, this is also how I feel about brushing my teeth.

Before my interview, I carefully laid everything out, including my now worn out discounted Ann Taylor Loft suit. I pulled out every file from previous jobs that I ever completed and picked out the best pieces to illustrate an example of each bullet in the job description to show I already had mastered a similar work task. I pulled out student worker projects, old emails I sent myself drunkenly of Brownward Mill projects the night of my great escape and brushed up on my sales analyst terms I long forgotten from ViewIt. There was a gaping hole in my resume from the current year I was spending napping on the couch, but I printed out every credible freelance article I had written and highlighted it as an example of my great writing skills that could be used when writing market reports.

I got ready in Bloomington and left in what I thought would be plenty of time to get to downtown Chicago. But such as with every time I want to go anywhere in the city, there was traffic. Why there would be gridlocked traffic on a random weekday in August, who knows. It was so bad I could have parked my car, hobbled along the shoulder of I-55 in my low slingback heels and probably would have made it faster than I did driving. I panicked and used my cunning driving skills to get from point A to point B, which was just me speeding down side streets and screaming swear words at the top of my lungs.

I originally planned to stop at my parents' house before I headed to the interview, but I was so insanely late that I had to go straight to DePaul and park. This would have been fine if I hadn't been wearing gym shorts and flip-flops. See, driving in a car for two hours makes your clothes wrinkly, so I thought it would be best to change right before to appear fresh and crisp. But I was running out of time. The interview was for 1:30 PM, and I had parked my car down the block at 1:20 PM, still in my flippy flops. I contemplated for one second changing in the car, but knowing my luck and penchant for horrifically awkward situations, I decided not to risk being seen by a potential future coworker. Instead, I ran inside one of DePaul's other buildings across the street from where I'd be interviewing. I bolted toward the doorman, asked him where the nearest bathroom was and dashed up the second floor. 1:23 PM, I FLUNG my work bag into the nearest stall, kicked off my flip-flops, pulled on my pantyhose, and zipped my Ann Taylor Loft skirt. 1:27 PM, I threw my gym shorts in a garbage bag, half stuffed it into my work bag, and ran across the street in my heels.

1:32 PM I was there, catching my breath. They say you're supposed to not rush into an interview, and you should arrive 15 minutes early to show you are reliable and on time. This, however, is not how I roll, so I plopped down in the lobby chair looking like I ran a 5K before entering the office. Joy came to get me minutes later, and I practically leaped in the air when I saw her. I was more confident then I had ever been in a nerve-racking situation, and I think that was the first sign that this was the right place for me. Plus, I kicked ass in the interview. Like, even if I came in wearing my shorts and flip-flops, they still would have hired me because my interview skills were on point.

I first got the email from Joy in May. Because my life isn't actually a Disney movie, I didn't get the job-until the end of summer. It took a while for everything to fall into place, but I waited it out and started what would be an amazing job that year.

When I first started writing this chapter, I was going to end it with something like, "and I lived happily ever! The end!" with 'the end' handwritten in big huge block letters, similar to how I would end all of my creative writing as a kid, possibly adding two exclamation points for dramatic effect. But because I am slightly superstitious, and because I have enough work history behind me to know better, I know I probably won't be at my wonderfully calm, meaningful job for the rest of my life. And that's fine; nothing lasts forever- if it did, I'd be a 30-year-old high school senior eating cookies in the cafeteria right now. Hopefully, though, it ends well. Preferably, I'd like to leave my last day by exiting on a unicorn, flying through the office, waving caring goodbyes to my coworkers as I toss them flowers made of candy, and they, in turn, cheers me with beer. That would be idyllic.

What's important right now is to have fun and enjoy the time while it lasts. For me that includes pranking coworkers, trying all the food trucks that park near my office building and adding things to the resume that make me look and feel like a marketing badass. That way, when it is time to leave, I will know I did not waste my time renting that unicorn.

When I Grow Up

THE DAY I REALIZED I was kind of an adult was at a benefit dinner for a business advocacy group at the Chicago Cultural Center. Going to a benefit or charity dinner is a telltale sign you are an adult. Think about it, pretty much every kid movie ever made starts out with getting rid of the parents at the beginning by having them attend a charity benefit, leaving the kids under-supervised by an incompetent bystander which allows the first point of chaos or exciting event to take place and jumpstart the plot. Perfect example: *Hook* with Robin Williams and that guy who played Richard, Monica's once love interest in *Friends*. Robin Williams plays a grown-up Peter Pan who is now an adult and heading off to a benefit at a hospital, which is when Hook (Richard, the guy with a mustache) came in and stole Peter's children, taking them to Never Never Land. In the getting ready to leave your children to fend for themselves scene, the mother always has on tights, high heels, and is wearing fancy jewelry, all of which I was wearing, thus further proving I was in the adult category.

Hold on. I just Googled '*Hook* the movie' to make sure I got the characters right, and Richard (who has a real name and calls himself Tom Selleck) totally wasn't in the movie. Apparently Dustin Hoffman played Hook? That's bizarre to me. Why didn't they have Tom Selleck play Hook? He already had a strong mustache. Although I will give credit to Hoffman for pulling off a fantastic Hook/Tom Selleck/Richard, it just would have made more sense to go with the obvious choice. As much as this is distracting from my original thought for the ending of this chapter, I am going to keep it in as symbolism for what adulthood is like: mostly confusing and very difficult to keep up with, and sometimes includes mustaches. Also, in adulthood you can chalk up every explanation with a bullshit excuse. Symbolism!

If you told me as a child I was going to have to attend these types of events someday I would have thrown myself onto my bed face down in agony. The reason is that I hated dressing up as a kid, as previously evidenced by my hatred for funeral attire, and also because when I was a kid, they never served good dressing at fancy events. It was always red French dressing or gross colorless Italian. Always! They never had my favorite, Ranch, and rarely did they serve Thousand Island, Ranch's second cousin. I'm happy to report that nowadays most places have smartened up and put some Ranch on the table for guests who have taste buds. I think if I ever have one of those Back to the Future-type moments with myself, the first thing I'm going to tell my chubby ten-year-old self is *Don't worry! Ranch dressing is now popular. And most of the time you can get away with leggings, which are WAY more comfortable than tights.* Then I would show myself pictures of me in bad haircuts so I could avoid that bowl cut with bangs in 5th grade.

So I was sitting inside this beautiful Chicago architectural building in all its glory, trying to ignore my inner child that wanted to stare up at the beautiful Tiffany glass dome ceiling. Unfortunately, it's not very adult-like to stare up at a ceiling in the middle of a presentation. Adults slightly tilt their heads as they swill a glass of wine in their hands; they don't stare wide-mouthed while a presenter is talking, no matter how boring the speech may be. Andrew and I were seated right in the center of a room among a group of people we didn't know. We were there because Andrew was on the board for the council. I was there to play the game "catch the wine servers eye as many times as you can while presentations of awards go on for nine hours." followed by the "When is the right time to go to the bathroom and how do I walk through this labyrinth of tables while someone is talking?" game. They're both fun, and I recommend playing them next time you are anywhere with presentations and wine.

We were in the latter half of the eighty-fifth hour of presenters, and I was torturing my bladder by sitting there. One of the presenters, a member of the council, had started his speech and started talking about the council, how it was formed, blah blah blah. But then he said something interesting that made me forget I had to pee. He said one thing that he does every once in a while is visualize where he will be in five, ten and twenty years and what his life will be like. He pictured himself in a cool red car, with a fancy lake house and season seats at Wrigley Field. Then he went on to boring stuff about how he envisioned the future of the council, so I checked out. But I thought it was an interesting exercise worth trying. What made it interesting was that he thought of fun things first, and left out the boring things like what if the car depreciates at a rapid speed, or whether he could write off the season tickets if he took his clients to the games and whether it was worth taking out a second mortgage on the lake house or not. Sitting there, being an adult-like person, I thought I should do that someday and sit down and write out what I would like my life to look like in the next five years.

And then I totally forgot about it and never did it. Because as an adult you forget stuff and you get busy with other things.

Luckily, this idea stayed in my head. So without further ado, my life as what I would like it to be like in the future when I am thirty-five-ish years old.

House

When I was younger, I used to want to live in a big mansion with all my friends. This was before the days of reality TV, where the premise for almost all shows is, "Let's stick people in a nice looking house together and make them hate each other." Thanks for ruining my dream, *Real World*.

Nowadays, I would like to have a row of mansions where I have all my close friends and family members living on the same block. It's genius because it eliminates driving time, yet you can run back home if you get bored or hungry. So we would all have a mansion next to each other, but I would totally still have a security gate because, you know, people can get annoying sometimes. That's when I unleash my set of hounds. But my hounds will be black labs like my dog

Chompers, and instead of attacking they will just run up to the gate and bark annoyingly while they jump in place, trying to get your attention in hopes that you will pet them.

The outside grounds of my mansion will have all of my favorite flowers and tons of fountains. Peonies, those purple flowers that I can't think of the name but look like they're from a Dr. Seuss book, and lilacs all over the place. I will develop a special area for insects and train them to stay in that area, away from where I will sit out and tan (I will also be magically able to tan and not burn in the future). There will be a pool of course, and a waterslide and a swim-up bar. But NO ONE can pee in the pool and if they do they have to sit in the insect forest and get eaten alive by mosquitoes.

Inside my mansion, I will have the following items:

- A Coca-Cola dispenser that replaces the water dispenser from the refrigerator.
- A mango margarita machine.
- An exact replica of the library in Beauty and the Beast, with the movie playing in the library at all times.
- A closet filled with outfits that are already put together, all of which make me look one million pounds slimmer.
- Comfortable chairs all over. There will be lots of chaises so I can collapse into a nap wherever I am, *including* the kitchen.
- An award shelf for all my writing awards, including the Nobel Peace Prize, and the MacArthur Grant in a new category for writing hilarious books, which was created especially for me.

- A tele-transporter that allows me to travel to any place in the world so I never have to stand in line at the airport ever again. (Sidenote: in editing, I realized that I could have just wished for a private jet. How poor am I that I don't even think of my own jet when I wish for things in the future?!)
- A full bathroom. (This one is just a placeholder in case a genie ever grants my wishes and I get some jerk that gets me on a technicality. "Here are your mansions! Oops- you didn't say it had to have a bathroom. Too bad." I'm on to you, imaginary asshole genie.)

Writing

In the very first chapter of this book, when I first lured you into reading the book of a mid-level marketing person who naps way too much and you are now slightly disturbed by her TV habits, I shared my vision of my book launch, where I would dance the night away in my black lace dress (A dress I purchased years ago to motivate me to lose weight. Did not work.) Afterward, I would go on a real book tour and travel to cities reading pieces of this book to adoring fans who would take me out to the bar and buy me drinks and eat pizza with me. I have contemplated entirely too much on what I will wear to these events. Possible ideas have included:

- Something related to the book, like white tights or my Luigi's black polo shirt and khakis.
- Yoga pants, which is what I wore writing the majority of this book.

- A big comfy infinity scarf (I don't know why exactly, but something about an infinity scarf says 'book tour' to me).

Then after all the glamor and pizza eating, I would travel to Washington D.C. with Andrew where I would go to the Library of Congress and find my book. I would then make him take a picture of me with the book. Then probably another one because he always takes pictures too fast without looking. Then we would probably get into a fight because I would yell he's not being sensitive enough to my big moment and he'll yell it's fine and can we just go because it's hot in here and he's starving. I look forward to it immensely.

Another first book-related thing I will be in awe of is having an ISBN number. To me, having that number will make it all feel real. It's like the social security code of books- if you have one you can never have it taken away because it is proof that it is real. Unless some other book comes around and steals mine, ruining this book's credit score, which would suck.

After that, I will write several more books but will keep my street cred by still working in marketing. Or am I just saying that so my boss doesn't fire me after reading this book because clearly I am a terrible employee? Who knows? Time will tell. (Please don't fire me).

Travel

I'm not a frequent traveler. As a kid, my parents took us to lots of wonderful places- Florida, Cape Cod, Pennsylvania, where we rode a train all the way from Illinois to experience the great scenery, and all I remember is that they had great microwavable cheeseburgers. I preface this next story by first starting out with the nice trips, because if I talk about the covered wagon festival without mentioning that we went on fun trips, my mom is going to yell at me for years saying, "I can't believe you wrote about the covered wagon festival and not the lovely trip to Cape Cod." Don't worry crazy lady; I mentioned Cape Cod!

My mom once took us to a covered wagon festival and it was the worst experience of my life followed by a moment of complete joy. For those of you who did not play Oregon Trail growing up as a kid, a covered wagon is what pioneers used to ride around in before they got typhoid and died. I was somewhere between the age of getting my hormones and full on teenager, 11 maybe, when her and my dad shuffled my sister and me to some random location in the Midwest in a big open field dedicated to covered wagons. I just searched for the location on the Internet, but all that comes up are some covered bridge festivals in Indiana. Those look like Lollapalooza compared to a covered wagon festival.

We arrived at the grounds after driving hours in I don't know what direction, and find ourselves in an open field with dead, brown grass as far as the eye can see. There was no shade, no place to sit and pout, and it was about 159 degrees. I don't remember seeing any wagons at all, only tables of overpriced crafts and locally grown produce and honey for sale. Perhaps if I were a more entrepreneurially spirited kid, I would have seen the items for sale and invented Whole Foods. I did not invent Whole Foods. Instead, I focused my eyes on something more important- the mysterious blue slushie.

Across the field of dead grass was a kid with a blue slushie. This caught my eye for two reasons. One, because the kid did not look like he was dying of heat, like I was, and two, because there were virtually no vendors or any food or drinks to be found, other than the cooler my dad had packed in the car, which was parked about 200 covered wagon lengths away (I'm guessing on the distance of course because like I said, there weren't any stupid covered wagons around).

Being notoriously shy, I begged my mom to find out where the blue slushie came from. It took some persistence since she was living it up at the fair, which to her really was Lollapalooza. But I had years of begging my mom to talk to strangers for me under my belt (I think I was in high school before I started ordering from waiters), so she finally caved. It turns out there was, and here's the kicker, a water park approximately 100 covered wagon lengths away from the festival. The irony of there being a water park next to a festival where my mom took us on a family vacation was lost on me for years. I must have repressed it until now. But with my sharpshooter-like focus and persistence, I wasn't even paying attention to the winding slides and lazy river. I just wanted that blue slushie. My mom obliged, probably because she realized how cruel and heartless she was for taking her kids to a hot field next to a water park for vacation, and bought me a blue slushie. And that is how I came to love covered wagons and their festivals.

Although I am not a worldly traveler, there are a few places I follow on Instagram that look pretty. The first is Ireland, the most beautiful looking country in the world. I'm in love with the country even though I have never stepped foot on it. Although, I do go to the

Milwaukee Irish Fest every year with my family where we spend the weekend drinking, eating and the best part-listening to Irish music. I assume Ireland is the same except they don't have fried food vendors everywhere. Or do they? If so, I'll never leave.

I also have never been west of Iowa, aside from Las Vegas, which doesn't count because Las Vegas isn't real. I would like to go to Oregon/Washington/all the places where the Twilight movies were filmed. Say what you want about those movies, but I never realized how beautiful the western part of the U.S. was until a vampire took a bad actress flying across the treetops just to get her out of his room. I also want to go there so I can see a giant waterfall. Actually, most of my destination locations are water-based. After the waterfall trip, I'd like to see a tide pool and a swamp. I think it's because I'm an Aquarius.

Random

There are several other aspects of my life I would like to sort out in the next five years. Here are a few of them.

1. I want to be able to order confidently at Starbucks.

Whenever I am in the morning line at Starbucks, my knees buckle, and I always crack under pressure of sensory overload and the fast-paced setting of it all. There are too many visuals up on that damn drink board for me to fall into a routine that makes sense. I can go in knowing very well that I want a Venti Pike with room, but one glance at a Caramel Frappuccino and I'm having coffee dessert for breakfast. I know what all the coffee words mean too. A Venti is a big kids cup, and a Grande is for when I'm not hungover. I honestly can't recall the name for small, but it's something that I will never need in my vocabulary. But even though I know all the words to form a Starbucks sentence, it always comes out like, "Can I have a hot drink that tastes good and won't burn my tongue, please? How many dollars do you want me to give you? Ok, thanks mister!" This might sound trite, but I think having confidence while ordering overpriced coffee drinks will help me bode confidence in other aspects of my life as well.

2. I want to do the monkey bars.

If I were ever in a situation where someone had to choose between another person and me to save because we were both hanging off a cliff, there would be no competition, because I would fall to my death immediately due to lack of arm strength. My arms are as weak as a Tyrannosaurus Rex. Much like a T-Rex, my arms are mainly for flailing around while I look angry, and nothing else.

I would like to develop enough arm muscle to be able to do all the arm exercises that I could never do in gym class. That includes the pull-up bar, the monkey bars, and the rope climb. Until then, I will be in my basement doing Jillian Michaels' 30 Day Shred poorly and hoping it will be enough for me to do at least one decent push-up before I die.

3. I want to be an IRONMAN.

I ran a marathon once, and it was the best day of my life. An Ironman (for those of you who haven't lost a remote while the TV was stuck on ESPN during the race coverage from Kona, Hawaii) is a triathlon race of swimming, biking and running to the extreme. The race starts with a 2.4 mile swim as your warm up. Then you dry off and hop on a bike for 112 miles. After that, you cool down with a full 26.2 mile marathon. My muscles cramp up just thinking about it. But I promised myself that the only way I can go to Hawaii is if I do an Ironman. Then I can go to Kona and watch the Kona race, which is where all the elite Ironman racers go to compete. If you're ever bored, and it's on one day, I highly suggest watching it. It has the Oprah-esque inspiration where you see people's stories of how they overcame insane obstacles to do a race that is absolutely batshit nuts to do. A nice metaphor for life, really.

4. I want to become a Swingin' Senior Chicago Bulls Dancer.

Someday, when I'm finally ready to retire from the marketing game, I would like to audition to become part of the greatest dance troupe ever: the Chicago Bulls' Swingin' Seniors dance team. You have to be over sixty years old, so luckily I have some time to practice, but when I grow up, I want to be on this team, dancing away during halftime to awesome oldies hits, which by then will be songs like Drunk in Love by Beyoncé.

So that is what I will be doing in the next few years. It's going to be pretty difficult; especially trying to find a way to do all this while lying on the couch, but hopefully, it will get done. Writing out my hopes and dreams for the future is somewhat liberating. It's a nice checklist to keep me going, and a nice stinging slap in the face when I don't get these things done. At the very least, it will be a good list to reference when I want to avoid other things. Oh, there's a family reunion, and those weird cousins are going to be there? Sorry! I'm going on book tour that weekend! Oh, you want me to help you move? Umm, that's when my new refrigerator with the pop dispenser is being installed, and I have to sign for it. This is brilliant. I should have set goals for myself years ago.

All in all, I think I just described the life of J.K. Rowling, but a poorer version because I'm not planning to have an amusement park based on my writings. I guess you could say I have low expectations for myself.

Random Words of Wisdom I Wanted to Leave You With Before I Leave This Meeting

- Don't scratch your boob at your desk, even if you are one thousand percent certain no one is going to walk by. They will, and it will be weird.

  o The same thing applies to plucking a chin hair.

- Don't eat out of the candy dish. It is a cesspool of hand germs. Buy some in the vending machine and don't share.

- Bring Christmas treats in if you like your coworkers. If not, buy some more candy and eat it by yourself.

- Don't look up the word 'girls' or any gender for that matter on the internet. Use stock photos for that PowerPoint instead. Trust me, Google Images is full of freaks.

- A hair straightener will work as an iron for that wrinkly blouse.

- In an emergency, Chapstick rubbed between the thighs will stop chafing when you are wearing a skirt without tights.

- Staples will fix a falling hem, popped button, and any tear in clothing that may present itself before an important meeting.

- Don't get involved in an office romance.

  o When you do get involved in an office romance, play it cool and don't tell anyone.

  o When you do tell someone about your office romance, make sure they're cool. Then get dirt on them so you have something to hold over them. This is called bonding with coworkers.

- Don't cry in the office.

  o Cry in the bathroom stall and say you have allergies.

- Steal all the office supplies!

- Do embezzle if you're sure you won't get caught.

- Be nice to the cleaning ladies and janitors; they are usually the nicest people in the office.

- Don't be the person who doesn't refill the coffee pot, doesn't replace the paper towels, or doesn't chip in enough for lunch.

- Try not to fart in the office.

- o Keep Febreze in your drawer for when you do fart.

- Splurge on the nice calendar that has all the sections to get your life in order.

  - o Don't rely on a calendar to get your life in order.

- Don't put up with shit from that one guy in the office. Ever.

- Make an office work friend so that you have someone to hang out with on your lunch break. Picking out sandwiches is a million times more fun with someone else.

- Write thank you notes. It's one of those things you have to do, but will only get noticed if you don't do it.

- Don't show off your boobs or your balls by wearing tight clothes. Save it for happy hour.

  - o DO NOT GO TO HAPPY HOUR.

  - o Try not to drink too much at happy hour.

- Don't chew your food too loudly, don't slurp soup at a meeting, and don't play your music so everyone can hear it.

- Don't be an asshole to your subordinates, and definitely don't call them your subordinates.

- Don't be the smelly person in the office. Just take a shower.

- Be super nice to the IT people, or learn how to update software on your own.

- Above all, don't be a douche.

Exit Interview

HOLY CRAP I MADE IT to the end! And so did you! Honestly, I didn't think this was going to get done. I've been sitting with the Excel sheet tab where I keep my word count opened for what seems like decades. In a few hundred more keystrokes I will be done with the longest project I have ever completed. I may cry. I may drink in celebration. I may forget to take the load of laundry out of the dryer before it wrinkles. You could say there's a lot going on right now.

Ending a job is never easy. You go into a new workplace thinking this might be the one that sees you through retirement. Aside from those super on top of it people who make five-year plans and stick to them, most of us don't know when or how we will end our job. Hopefully, it's by choice, and if it's not, there should be lots of drinking and swearing involved. On the chance one does leave on peaceful terms, it's usually best to end things nicely with your soon-to-be former employer, even if they are the sole reason you are leaving. For me, I have reached the point in this job where it is time to move on.

When I started this project, I was in my brand new discounted Ann Taylor Loft suit. Now, I sit in your office in leggings that I am poorly passing off as work pants, a slouched light summer sweater that hangs off my shoulder, my hair in a messy bun, and my open-toed sandals propped up on your desk. Let's start this exit interview, shall we?

How did you like your time working for us?

This was without a doubt the most intensely difficult/fun/self-deprecating/awesome job I have ever had. It started out very confusing for me. I had no clue where to start, and no one left a set of instructions for me. But I think I figured things out, and now have almost eighty-thousand words to show for it. Not too shabby, eh?

Were your job responsibilities characterized correctly during the interview process and orientation?

God no. No one tells you how difficult it is to be a writer. I knew I wanted that J.K. Rowling money, but I had no idea how hard it was to write a book. In the end, it was worth it, even though I have yet to successfully pull off the "I'm a writer working on my first book" line at parties. Most people think I'm making it up.

Also, I think I broke the Keurig machine because nobody showed me how to refill it and now it won't stop beeping.

Where will your next position be?

If I'm lucky, I'll be back to do another book. I have lots of ideas, and even have a cool idea for a funny movie. Hopefully, if he's willing, the role of me will be played by Mr. Tom Hanks, my favorite actor.

If you could change anything about your time here, what would it be?

I would have written faster and spent a hell of a lot less time on Facebook. But I don't regret using up all the copy paper printing out drafts and eating the last doughnut in the breakroom. And as much as I love Chompers sitting at the feet of my desk as I write, I really could have done with fewer dog farts.

Is there anything else you wish to share before we part ways?

One more quick story before I go, then I really should be getting back to my actual job. Come to think of it, I haven't done any real work in months. I bet they're wondering what I've been doing here all this time.

Last winter I was particularly down in the winter blues. It was too cold to go out, I was too lazy to use the company treadmill, and I was all together feeling blah. I had however been going to Zumba on Saturdays with my friend Emily, where we would follow along to our instructor, the most energetic human being I have ever met. Although my dance moves mirror that of a little kid at a family wedding (mostly, jumping in place and screaming), I still leave every time feeling completely energized and excited for the rest of the day.

Sitting in my office one day, I was slumped over my keyboard with one hand on the mouse and the other on my chin, not even pretending to look like I was doing actual work. I was so sluggish and tired after lunch that I contemplated shutting my office door and taking a nap on my desk. But instead, out of nowhere, I decided to exercise. I had a 10-minute printout of exercises that required one minute of arm moves, followed by one minute of cardio, and repeated until all 10 moves were done. I grabbed a weight from my health-conscious coworker who kept weights at his desk, shut my door, and put my headphones on to listen to my underused yet upbeat exercise playlist.

The first minute of cardio was confusing. Fearful that the office would hear me jumping around, I decided that stepping in place was enough cardio to start. On round two I moved at a quicker pace, putting more hip thrust into it. Then, on round three, "Spice Up Your Life" by the Spice Girls came on, and the Zumba moves came out of me. By round four, when Scary Spice told me to slam it to the left, I was moving my ass to the side. When she told me to shake it to my right, I shook my hips with all my might, followed by a merengue-step to the front. I was a dancing fool by the end of the exercise rounds, dancing to glorious hits such as Missy Elliot's "Pass the Dutch," Beyoncé's "Get Me Bodied," and Fall Out Boy's "Dance, Dance." When my 20 minutes were up, I was smiling in my office, something I don't usually do after 3 PM when I'm stuck under fluorescent lights.

So although this may be the last time we meet for a little while, I hope our paths cross again soon. And in the meantime, send funny emails to me often, use up those vacation days, and when the opportunity strikes, always take the time to put on your music and have some fun.

ACKNOWLEDGMENTS

Whenever I would buy a CD, the first thing I would do after destroying my nails ripping open the packaging was read the album dedications. So I'd like to start this out like a 90's rapper dropping their first single. "I'd like to thank my producers, my family, my boo- baby you're the greatest. And Jesus, much love for giving me this talent right here! West Coast!"

And now for a few others that I'd like to include.

First, I want to thank my parents. Mom and Papa, you two are the best in the world. You did the impossible task of raising a human being who has less neurotic tendencies than the average person. Thank you for making me normal and happy and a million other things. Caitlyn turned out pretty OK too!

Caitlyn, I love you. You are the best little big sister I could ever have. Thank you for letting me pretend to be the better sister. Also, thank you for learning to chew with your mouth closed, you are the best sister for this and this alone.

Andrew, my husband, I love you more than Chompers loves eating paper. You are an amazing father and Millie is so lucky to have you as her Papa. Chompers, not so much. Also, thank you for taking out the garbage all the time. You're welcome for the clean underwear.

Alicia, Carolyn, Emily. Thank you for being examples of smart, successful, supportive, and non-bitchy women. I can't wait until we are old and can all retire, drink wine during the day at each other's houses and then nap. Five more years!

I'd like to thank all the nice teachers I've had over the years, especially the ones who helped me learn to love reading and writing and numbers. Ms. Bekier, Sr. Rosaline, Ms. Smith, Ms. Wolf, Ms. Zettle, Ms. Alfafara, Mrs. Bott, Ms. Tesauro, Zafar, Dr. Whalen, you made my brain bigger, so thank you for that.

Thank you to all the coworkers who I've enjoyed shooting the shit with over the years. There are too many to name, but if I ever plopped my butt down in your office chair, sat next to you on purpose in a meeting, or instant messaged you a joke, thank you for being awesome. You made the 40+ hour work weeks bearable, and I hope you read this book during the work day and stick it to the company by not getting anything done all week.

Thank you to Auntie Di and the entire Castellucci family, Mrs. Abuela and Ana for keeping me well fed and cared for. I love you all!

Alex, Anna and Ivann, thank you for not being weird in-laws and for remembering every February that not everyone likes banana cream pie. Much love.

Leo and Luca- you are my favorite nephews in the whole, wide world! I love you!

Some people have on more than one occasion asked me how this book was coming along, which was really nice of them. Thank you Sal, Eric, Ali, Nathan, Hazel, Cherry, Ana, Coleen, Jasmine, and Steph!

To my best friend Gwen. Your mom and dad have been so supportive and encouraging to me throughout the entire process of this book. You better be a good kid and never disobey them, or else you are going to hear from Nonnie!

Oh Chompers. My best friend, my first baby. I love you so much I just want to squish your face. You taught me how to be a mom and for that I am eternally grateful. But, you can't read, so I will buy you some dog treats.

And most importantly, to my Millie May. You weren't alive yet when I wrote this book, but I am so happy to be your Mommy and I can't wait to write down all the wonderful things you do so I can make another book, because parenting books sell like hotcakes

ABOUT THE AUTHOR

Connie O'Reyes is a humor writer who most notably gained recognition for her online column, Marathon Missfit, chronicling her start as a runner to the finish line of the Chicago Marathon, which appeared in the Chicago Tribune's Redeye. Her favorite snack to eat while writing is Twizzler Cherry Bites- not the strawberry ones.

If you loved this book, please let her know on Amazon, Goodreads, or at connieoreyes@gmail.com

Made in the USA
Monee, IL
22 December 2022

23325869R00166